# Mumpreneur on Fire

MUMS IN BUSINESS ASSOCIATION

# DEDICATION

To our children.

Kian, Kye, Enna, Olana, Elis, Jed, Obi and Poppy

Always know that you are capable of anything…..
And we love you more than you will ever know!

# ACKNOWLEDGEMENTS

There are so many women who have supported us on this crazy journey so far.

Firstly, from the bottom of our hearts we thank each and everyone of the amazing women who have shared their stories of inspiration.

Nanny Jill, I do not know what I would do without you. My number 1 fan...I love you x

Mum, You have no choice but to be stuck with me...but You do have a choice to believe in me. Thank you for not laughing when I told you I'd be famous one day!

Jane and Uncle Andy, You never doubted me even at my lowest points. Thank you for always being there!

Danielle, Nealie, Hayley, Sally, Megan and Skye. Without you guys to take the piss out of me I would have gone insane. Thank you for making me laugh when I wanted to cry.

Anne, Thank you for being like a mum to me.

To my Hubby Lee, Thank you for standing by me through everything.

Grandpa and Granny Fran, thank you for sticking by me when things got tough.

In June 2017 sisters Leona Burton and Estelle Keeber decided to create a group for Mums in Business. Being Mums in business themselves, they knew that there was a lack of support online and in the real world. And so Mums in Business Association was born! The response to the group was astronomical with members joining at a rate of up to 400 women per day!

Inside MIBA you can find amazing support networks, business advice and trainings as well as 1 to 1 coaching on all things MIB! With over 17 thousand members you are sure to find the support or advice that you are looking for whether you need help with growing your sales or dealing with tantrums!

MIBA is a platform for women and mums from all over the globe to grow their businesses and have a happier healthier life.

Leona and Estelle hope to inspire and support millions more women to take control of their destiny and dream BIG!

This book shares the inspirational stories of 20 of the members of MIBA. Reading these stories will show you that with dedication and hard work anything is possible, even against all odds!

You can find more information about Mums in Business association on the website:

www.mumsinbusinessassociation.com

# CONTENTS

# 1. AYESHA

My name is Ayesha Hashim, I am 30 years old. Mother of two amazingly active boys, full time student at the open university, Tefl teacher and entrepreneur. I think it's safe to say that my life is very hectic; I am the eldest of ten children so responsibility is a big part of my life, so here's my story on how overcame the deep inner self-doubt, a battle with drugs and alcohol through family support and sheer determination. I was born in Mogadishu in Somalia, on January 1st,1987 to mum Fowsia and father Hashim, we moved to London when I was two years old. My parents went on to have seven other daughters. From a young age, I was aware of how strong my mum was. My mum came to England with just me and my sister with no other support system, I'd never seen someone so organised, who worked well under so much pressure. My dad on other hand, who was usually away would always find some way to disturb the peace, constantly accusing my mum and putting her down. My mum stayed strong and made sure we were protected, ensuring that we enjoyed our childhood. As I grew and entered secondary school, I started to notice that girls weren't nice and I began to get picked on. For months, girls would laugh at me, make fun of how I looked by calling me names, pulling my chair when I was sitting, kicking me under the table. The bullies made me feel so ashamed that I kept my bullying a secret, I would frequently pretend I was sick so I could be excused from classes that I shared with those girls. All this caused me to act out and start rebelling at home. My mum noticed a change in me and decided to move schools which made me feel better. Not long after I left the school, we moved to Birmingham and after we had settled in mum decided that she'd had enough and filed from divorce. So now my mum was a single mum of eight girls, ages ranging from 13 to 1 years, which is a lot. I honestly do not know how she did it. Somehow, she had us all in private schools, made sure we were dressed in the best clothes and ate wholesome and organic foods. By this point, I had made lots of friends who were the wrong kind of friends, it is here that I now know that I just wanted to feel accepted by my peers and I was constantly seeking approval for that. It was not until 2017 that I really became aware of the extent that I was seeking approval.

After a year of mum being single, she met my step-dad and they had two children making our family complete with ten children. My mum had nine girls and one boy who was the youngest so our house was a full house and constantly noisy. Throughout secondary school I continued to get worse, becoming one the most popular girls at my school which made me feel invincible so I would always cause trouble and be disruptive. But being the centre of attention wasn't enough for me, I was just getting worse and worse. My grades continued to plummet to an all-time low and I began to skip school on a regular basis, getting suspended for fighting in school, upsetting teachers. It was at this point that I realised that I was becoming exactly like the bullies that I despised but I couldn't stop. It was a vicious cycle of make trouble, hear advice from mum, feel somewhat remorseful and repeat. I failed my GCSE's due to lack of concentration on school work and not being in school a lot. I felt like a failure and I never forgave myself for that. I started running away from home and causing my mum immense heartache and stress, it was like I was oblivious to the destruction was creating around me. I wanted to stop but I couldn't.

At the age of 16, to try to turn my life around decided to get married to a man from London who was 19 at the time. I convinced my mum and step-dad that I was ready to get married as premarital relations are forbidden in our religion. After some deliberation, his mum and his brother came to meet with my family. The pre-wedding arrangements were completed quite quickly and before I knew it was the day of my wedding. I was so nervous but I ready to start a new life, one where I was a grown up. The wedding was a small, close family occasion, where we celebrated it as a new chapter in our lives, a clean slate. After the wedding was done, I was anxious to leave Birmingham and relocate to London. My husband and I planned to stay with his mum until we got our own flat. My mother-in-law seemed nice enough so I didn't really have any issues with staying with them. The first few days were great, we ate out, took so many romantic walks around central London, our special spot was Primrose Hill. My new husband was one of the kindest, most generous and funny man I'd ever met, I adored him but I was finding it hard to bond with his mother; it was as if she resented me. As time went on I felt a very negative vibe in the house, it just wasn't peaceful anymore. I had no idea what the problem was, and the harder I tried, the worse it got. Apparently, I didn't cook or clean to her "standard", she put me down at every opportunity. She caused some major problems between my family and me. It got to a point where I lost contact with my family, it was a devastating blow to me. I loved my family but I just didn't know what was real anymore, I loved my husband and I wanted to make it work.

We were only married a year and there were so many cracks and warning signs which I ignored, I didn't want to admit defeat. In 2006, my Husband got a job as an English teacher in Jeddah, Saudi Arabia. We were so excited and couldn't wait for that chapter in our lives and I just wanted to be away from my mother-in-law. By this point I was an empty shell of my former bubbly self; I had no opinion, I couldn't even say no to anything and I was just existing. I cried myself to sleep every single night, I hadn't spoken to my family in 18 months, was very suicidal and contemplating overdosing on pills. I was having a breakdown. After my husband had left to start his job and sort my visa out, things got darker. I was sinking further and further in a deep depression and nothing seemed real. I felt disgusted in myself for not speaking out in situations when I should have spoken out, not reaching out to my family to make amends but so much time had passed and I was so terrified that it was too late. I mean, I'd hurt my mum on so many levels, here I was with people who didn't value me or care for me and for what? I was beating and blaming myself about everything daily, in my mind, I was worthless, uneducated, had nothing to offer. I was nothing. The nights were the worst, it was something about the silence that filled me with sadness. By this point, my take on life was extremely negative, over analysing every single situation but throughout all things troubling me, I had hope. A strong hope that overrode everything, a kind of hope that told me that this temporary, you'll get your family back, you'll be okay, I mean you're not dying, right? I had strength within me but it was trapped, how do I let it out? When will I ever be free? These questions would be swimming around in my head constantly. Just when I was on the brink of insanity, my visa came through, I was ecstatic to be leaving England. A couple of days later I embarked on my new journey to Saudi Arabia, I was a bank of emotions, sad, angry, shame, excitement and happiness. I cried the whole flight over there which a long six hours but I determined to fix everything with my family, but that wasn't meant to be yet. Living in Saudi Arabia was a dream, it was a life that I'd never seen, my husband had a great job and we had tons of fun. We'd regularly do activities like romantic dinners, go to the theme park, have tea at the beach and go snorkeling. We are starting to bond again and it was fun but I was missing my family. I needed my mum. Again, I felt dark and this was when I started smoking like a chimney, one after other. I joined a gym to take my mind of things but I just wanted to hide away. I stopped cleaning, working, cooking and basically gave up on myself. I told myself that I was worthless, I didn't deserve happiness and that my family were better off without me. In August 2006, I started to feel sick and was hospitalised for kidney stones, I was in excruciating pain and I just wanted my mum but that wasn't an option so I took that feeling and put it in my ever-growing bank of emotions. After spending a couple of days in hospital, I returned home, it was like I was living in an unknown world. I hardly recognised myself and who I was becoming.

About 3 weeks later, I was still feeling sick and I did a pregnancy test, it was negative. I had a mix of emotions, I was happy and sad. One week later in September 2006, I did another test and it was positive. I cried my eyes out, I wasn't sure why I was even crying. As my bump grew I was falling deeper into depression, it was so bad that I wasn't sure what was real or fake. In December 2006, I decided to come back to England to have my baby. I was 6 months pregnant and an emotional wreck. I came back to England alone crying all the way back. Seeing my mother-in-law made me sick and I knew that I needed to change things. She was worse than before, I was useless and confused. A couple of weeks later my husband came back to the UK, which felt bittersweet because although I was happy to see him, I knew things were bad.

As time went on things got worse, I could tell this wasn't going to work and something about becoming a mother was taking me in another direction. I was ready to make some changes but I didn't know where to start, my family, my mental state. On Easter Sunday 8th April 2007, the love of my life was born. I couldn't believe that I was a mum. This little being was trusting me wholeheartedly with his life. I had never felt a love like this, my son, who I named AbdulKarim, was my world. During the next few weeks, I kept my head my head down and finally decided to move back to Birmingham. I had to take charge of my life. So, when Abdulkarim was 8 weeks old, I went back to Birmingham. I was one of the hardest things ever, to try and rebuild my life. My family were very open hearted, and welcomed me with open arms. The aftermath of everything was really starting to get to me, I couldn't sleep, I was having nightmares and regular panic attacks. I was staying with mum and was overwhelmed with joy to be back, however, I was finding it difficult to cope with everything. I slowly falling again. In September 2008, I moved out of my mum's house to my own flat, which was kind of like supported accommodation. At first, it was good and I was doing well, I was organised and enjoyed living alone with my little baby. I was divorced, young and had a new outlook on life. I ready to do better and be better. Most of my neighbours were all young mums and I started to bond with them as we had shared interests. As time passed I began drinking regularly and smoking weed to cover up how I was feeling inside. I was so scared of thinking clearly because that meant I would have face all the issues I'd been running away from. Amidst all this self-destruction, I enrolled in college to do sociology and psychology as well as doing anything else that was free that I could get me hands on.

In July 2009, I met a guy who, I wouldn't have even looked at twice, but I was at a low place in my life, I went for it. This guy was not good for me, he would put me down, basically treating like the worthless girl I had been telling myself that I was. Things continued to get worse and I completely despised myself. By 2011, I was unrecognisable, my son was always at my mums so I could do what I wanted. I loved my mum and family but the pull of drugs was pulling me stronger. I walked out on everyone including my son. It pains to even say or think about this. I was in breakdown mode and I wouldn't even go outside. My days were a cycle of get high, come down from that, cry and repeat. I was bullied daily by the guy I was with.

Here I was again, I'd isolated myself from my family but I was to blame fully. I had nothing, everyone was better off without me. I was nothing and all I did was let people down again and again. There was no going back and it was just getting harder and harder.

At the beginning of 2012, just when I thought I was coming to the end of my life, my sisters came and rescued me from the situation. I will never forget that and I will be forever grateful for it. I was back at home starting again; I'd missed so much of my son's life. I had to get it together for him. I ended up relapsing for a couple of weeks in August 2012 but that was the last straw. In September 2012, my family decided enough was enough and encouraged me to go and stay with my uncle in Zanzibar, Africa to sort my head out. That trip changed my outlook on things and reminded me that nothing is final. I can change things. Little old me, I can do it. After spending three months there and no drugs or alcohol, it was time to come home, I missed my baby and my family. At the airport before boarding, I met a guy at security, he was nice and he helped me with everything. We exchanged numbers and boarded my plane. Back at home, I felt brand new but I was still carrying a horrible feeling with me that kept surfacing from time to time. I wasn't well. So, in April 2013, I went back to Zanzibar and spent almost 7 months there and the guy I met at the airport a few months earlier, we ended up getting married. We have now been married four years and we have a son together who's 3. I am so happy that I am finally taking charge of my life.

When I got back to England in November 2013, I made actual changes and for the first time ever wasn't just talking about change, I WAS doing it. For the next few months I kept my head down, focused on praying and getting stuck in with the family. I dropped contact with anyone that brought me down and anyone who reminded me of that careless girl I once was, the drug dealers, friends who liked to drink etc. In May 2014, when I had my second son, Ayman, I was determined to stay strong and become the woman my boys deserved. I decided that my family deserved more, my mum deserved more. My family picked me up when I was at my lowest, gave me chance after chance. Every time I messed up, my mum thought of a better way to help me. She will never know how much she means to me. I was becoming a new woman, I was so ready to leave all the past behind. I started on the grueling journey to self-discovery, I started praying on time, asking God for help. I woke up every morning and plugged in something positive and told myself that I have every reason to be proud. I beat my drug and alcohol addiction by taking all the help my family offered me, sharing my true feelings with my mum and staying honest with myself. It's been almost 5 years and I have come a long way.

The biggest lesson I have ever learnt over the years is to never give up on yourself, we all make mistakes. We are all learning. In 2015, I discovered personal development and that changed my life. Every day I would watch inspirational videos and read books that made me feel amazing. I started to change the way I spoke to people and more importantly how I spoke to myself. I have met some incredible women online that have helped me to grow as a woman and do things that I would've never done before. I have worked with a company that strived to uplift women and that made me realise that it's my passion to remind women how precious they are. We are badass and we need to remember that. I now create daily reminders for women who want to step into their light and fix their crowns via Facebook and Instagram. I have also learnt how important it is to invest in myself, I started working with a badass coach to get my sass back at the beginning of this year and I can't believe the personal breakthroughs I've had. I have trained myself to do better and be better, I am so grateful for what I have now. An amazing supportive family, a nice home, an incredible husband and an army of badass babes who will support me in whatever I choose to do. What more could a girl want?

Although I'm still at the start of journey to fully becoming the woman I want to become, I know I am on the right track. I have some amazing things planned for the next few years which reminds me that all that pain was worth it. Every single second of it. I am finally in love with me.

# 2. CIARA

My name is Ciara. I'm a daughter, a sister, a mother, a SUICIDE SURVIVOR. I have had mental health issues for as long as I can remember. I was always an awkward child and really nervous. I didn't fit in much and I found it hard to keep friends. I found it difficult to talk to people and kept a lot of my issues quiet. To the outside world I was just "rare".

My parents' breakup sent me into a spiral of depression when I was 11 or 12 and I went into my teenage years feeling so alone and broken. Most people know so it's no big secret to write it, but my father was a serious alcoholic and I took it upon myself to try and be a career to him after the breakup. I thought he would be really alone now without us and if I just got him sober I could save him and he could come home. Needless to say that was not how it all played out. No 12 year old will ever be emotionally equipped to try and sober up anyone with an addiction. I didn't fit in at school and was bullied really badly by several different people and with the problems going on at home it all just got too much. At this stage I'd made a couple of friends but we had moved house and it made it difficult for me to see them, so I was lonely once again and feeling like I didn't belong in this world.

At the age of 13 I was an absolute wreck. I didn't have a clue who I was or where I fit in and it was horrible. I was different and my friends knew it. I didn't like smoking and I got drunk just to be more socially accepted and I hated it. (I also got caught straight out and I thought the wrath of my mother would never be worth that again so my new found popularity was short lived.) They used to tease me about how weird I was and although they probably meant no harm I'd go home at night, put on my radio and cry myself to sleep. I hated me. I was so insecure and helpless. Music was my only therapy and I'd lose myself in the melodies.

One Saturday I had just had enough. I'd had a terrible week. People at school were still being awful and my friends were still calling me weird all the time and I was fed up with always being a social outcast, an anxiety ridden loser and an emotional punch bag. So I went downstairs took every single tablet we had in the cabinet and went to bed. I lay there for a few hours and I started to feel really sick. I could hear Brookside on the TV downstairs so I knew it must be 5pm at least. I closed my eyes and tried to sleep. This was not a cry for help. I wanted to die. I told nobody. I didn't change my mind or try to be sick or panic at all that I'd actually done this. I just lay there. All of a sudden I had to be sick so I ran to the bathroom. That must have been when I blacked out because I remember nothing else. I will believe in angels until the day I do actually die for this next turn of events. My friends from my old street randomly decided to surprise me and had walked all the way to my new house and knocked on the door. My mum let them in and they found me on the bathroom floor out cold. They got my mum and rang an ambulance and got me to hospital.

I woke up in hospital to my parents, brother and sister looking like they had just been through the most traumatic and soul destroying experience of their lives. The doctor told me had my friend found me ten minutes later she'd have found me dead. The look on my poor mother's face still haunts me to this day and the sound of my sister crying and the feeling of how tight she was gripping me as she hugged me still makes me want to cry. Seeing the aftermath of a suicide situation and the affect it has on the people who love the victim was awful. Knowing how much it scarred them emotionally. How much I'd shook the ones who loved me to the very core made me feel awful. I thought about how much worse their faces would have been had I succeeded. It was in that moment that I realised just what suicide did. I may have been "relieving" myself of my problems, but I'd almost handed my family an entire life sentence.

What happened over the next couple of years changed my entire world. I moved school, I made amazing new friends and I started to get more confident. I gave birth to the most amazing little girl who absolutely set my soul on fire. She literally saved me in so many ways. She taught me real, honest, true, unconditional love. Things were pretty peachy for a while, a few years in fact. We weren't without our struggles, I was still a teenage mum and money was tight, but thankfully I had my dad and our little life was perfect. He'd got sober for good and was an amazing help. We lived together, just the three of us in our little home. But life, as it does, deals us a blow that hits us so hard and my dad got cancer. I cared for him with my sister and my aunt for three years and as much as he fought to his last breath, he lost his battle six years ago.

My mental health issues were back and stronger than ever and I slipped into a depression so dark that I couldn't even function. My anxiety was so bad and I felt like I'd become a shadow of my former self. By this stage though, I'd met someone who I thought was amazing and we moved in together and got engaged. I set up my little hair salon in our house and things were fab. Or so I thought. I lost my granny quite suddenly and she's the only grandparent I'd ever known, she was also my dad's mum. I slipped again and my heart was so heavy. I knew my fiancé and I had our problems but I wasn't prepared at all when he finished the relationship out of the blue and moved out. In the following months I couldn't afford the rent, so I lost the house and in turn my little salon. I moved to a smaller place and put all of the money I had left into opening an actual salon. Things were pretty ok again for about 10 months. I was heartbroken, but I was moving forward. Cue Christmas 2014, when I lost my dad's brother and sister four days apart two weeks before Christmas, suddenly to heart attacks. We buried one on the Monday and one on the Friday. These two were like an extra set of parents to me and my whole world was shook once again.

In the meantime I'd gotten into a really toxic rebound relationship and my anxiety was through the roof. I had never been so low. My self-esteem was shot and I felt so worthless every day. I let him make me feel like I was nothing. I didn't have the strength to leave. I needed someone. I could kick myself looking back at that. I couldn't cope or function and I spiraled into what I can honestly say were the darkest days of my life so far. I lost the salon in the January and I started to cut off my friends and family. I was a horrible person and I didn't recognise myself in the mirror. I hated myself and I hated my life and I hated God and heaven and the universe for taking all that I'd held so dear. One of the friends who I'd cut off had always been there for me in times of need. She was your typical honest friend who'd always be there with a good kick into touch and some tough love and I started to really miss her. She was also my cousin and so I knew as much as she'd be angry she'd have to forgive me! I was back on my meds and was feeling much better so I got in touch to say " Hey I've been an absolute nightmare I'm sorry I haven't been in touch", to which she replied with a big lecture and an offer of lunch on the Saturday. I was so happy to be meeting up with her and was really looking forward to the weekend. I got a phone call on the Friday morning to say she had been killed in a car accident on the way to work. To this day it's the worst call I have ever received and it will haunt me until my last breath. I drank myself silly for about two months after, the guilt consuming me every day. I wanted to switch places. She was outgoing, beautiful, funny and really had her life together. An amazing job, lots of friends, a fantastic boyfriend, she had lived life to the max every day and made the most of everything. yet she was robbed of life and here I was wasting mine. It wasn't fair. I was an absolute loser, it should have been someone like me, not her.

When I finally sobered up and got a grip I had the most amazing epiphany. Life is not guaranteed. It's not ours to keep, it's on loan. We don't know when we will be called back and my goodness did I know this only too well with the amount of loss I had coped with in the past four years. Something woke up inside me and I decided enough was enough. I got out of that toxic relationship two years ago and I went back to school and met the most amazing people, who made me realise that my mental health issues and how I handled them were inspirational enough to make a career out of and I've just this year founded redesign your vibe, my high vibe mind set and anxiety coaching business based around helping people with mental health or self-esteem issues move forward fearlessly! The amount of people I have helped so far in the short length of time I've been doing this makes me cry my eyes out on a daily basis and I know that there's so many more people who will survive and go on to do amazing things because of me! That makes my heart so incredibly happy and humbles me to the very core of my being.

My girl has just celebrated her 16th birthday. She finishes her last year of school in May and we are off to travel around Europe. Had I succeeded in taking my life she would not be in this world. And if you've ever met my Aimee, girl you'd know what a massive loss to this world that would be. I have 11 amazing nieces and nephews, two who would barely remember me and 9 who would never have met me. I can't even fathom not knowing these amazing kids and watching them grow. Some of them are adults now with their own kids. I love them so much, more than life itself and they know if they ever need anything I'm there in a heartbeat.

I have had an amazing 14 year hair and makeup career. I have come so much out of my shell. I'm a positive force to be reckoned with. I am outgoing, successful and I have amazing friends. I love me. And I love my life. I've spent a year in London and it's been amazing! I've met some inspirational, fantastic people and I have acquired the skills I need to really go for gold! My life is mine to live. It's up to me to do good or let it pass me by. I will not waste even one more second.

The moral of this story is this... When you are at the end of your rope, tie a knot and hold on!!!! TALK. REACH OUT. SEEK HELP. Because even though now at this moment it looks like you have no other way out, believe me, if you just hold on for one more day, what lies ahead of you will be phenomenal. It's always darkest before the dawn, but I promise you, beautiful mental health warrior, if you fight on, the sun will shine again and it will shine so flipping bright that it will fill your heart with love!

You will look back at this time in your life and be proud of what an absolute SURVIVOR you are. You matter what. Your life matters and people love you. If I can do this, then so can you! You can be, do and have anything that you set your mind on in this life. You just have to believe. Believe in you, believe you deserve it. Because you do!

The future holds amazing things for my brand and soon everyone will know its name, because I won't stop until they do. I plan to help every single beautiful soul I can along the way. Anyone who tells you that dreams don't come true is lying. Go get yours today lady!

# 3. DENISE

Let's start from being a single mum. A point I know so many women are currently at. Let me tell you this should only fire up the passion in your belly even more. Prove to yourself and everyone else that you can do it!

I became a single mum when my daughter was 21 months old and my son was just 8 months old. Thankfully I'd already bought my first house before marrying so I could provide my children with a stable home and a roof over their head. That was until one night only 6 months after my marriage split, a horrendous storm sucked the gable end out of our house, leaving me and my children homeless overnight. Thankfully I have a loving family who took us in for the nine months it took for the house to be repaired and rebuilt. Single mum life can be tough. Yes I've done the whole reduced to clear shop! One Christmas was really tough and I made most of my children's toys myself. A castle and a dolls house out of cardboard boxes. Which at 2 and 3 years old they obviously absolutely loved to bits! I've always had a very strong positive outlook on life and am hugely grateful for everything in it. So I never looked at being a single mum as a negative thing always a positive one. No more sweaty sock washing for me! I stayed good friends (and still am) with my ex-husband. But it wasn't easy at time when our children were little as he lived and worked at the other end of the country from us so wasn't able to lend a helping hand regularly. One thing that has always been constant in my life though are my two best friends, strong females who have always supported me through all my crazy adventures and there have been a few!

Once my children were settled in school I had a variety of 9-5 jobs. Everything from shoe shops to supermarkets. I even did half a day in a toilet roll factory. Half a day was enough believe me! But building success for someone else wasn't my idea of a great future. I then found a job that was ok and I worked when my children were at school, then in the evening once they were in bed my mum came over whilst I went to night school to study Biology, Chemistry, Physics and Holistic therapies. Don't be impressed by the physics though I was rubbish at it! It was tiring let me tell you. Then the company I worked for was bought out and my new manager arrived! He was overbearing and arrogant. I really started to dislike my job. Just as I had passed all my courses my manager announced the company was struggling and asked for voluntary redundancies. My hand has never shot up as quick in my life! I received a redundancy package. Took a leap of faith and opened my own Holistic Therapy Clinic. I remember the first week the only People through the door were the postman and a delivery driver bringing in my Essential oils. So I took my show on the road and asked friends to have pamper parties for me which helped me build up the start of a regular client list. If clients don't come to you go out and find them! After a bit of a slow start things started to take off and my client list grew. Soon my diary was regularly full. I'd developed treatments using fresh ingredients as well as essential oils. Some of the most popular ones being avocado, lemon and strawberry facials. Honey butter and cucumber body polish. Rose and frankincense milk body glow. My clients were treated with robes, slippers and a relaxation room for after their treatments too.

Being a therapist is hard work physicality so the last thing I wanted to do was go home and cook. So, much to the delight of my children we ate out most nights. I think it's great to set that success comes with rewards for hard work. After a few years my health took a bit of a wobble and I kept passing out. Not the best thing when you're running a business. It turned out I was extremely anaemic and I needed an operation that would put me out of action for at least 6 months. So I had to make a tough decision to sell my clinic. It didn't take long to find a buyer. But it was really hard letting go. After only a week the lady who bought it rang me in a panic crying that she couldn't cope and was overwhelmed by the workload. It's funny when I look back as I immediately contacted another lady who had also wanted to buy the clinic from me. She then jumped at the chance and bought the clinic from the previous lady and I gasped a sigh of relief for all of my valued regular clients. Even though the business was no longer mine I still had a great sense of customer care. Once you have that I don't think it ever leaves you. After some time out and recovery my business nose was twitching again! This time my journey took a different path.

I'd previously visited and fell in love with a picturesque town called Hebden Bridge in West Yorkshire. It wasn't just my business nose that was twitching though, but my gypsy feet too. So after some planning and sourcing I opened a gift shop in Hebden Bridge with my cousin. I loved it from day one and enjoyed getting to know some of the local characters in this quirky town. After about a year my cousins heart wasn't in it anymore so she decided to leave and I carried on running the shop on my own. As fate would have it I'd taken in a couple of pieces of painted furniture and done a few myself. Theses started to sell really well and after a time my gift shop transformed into a Shabby Chic furniture shop. It got really busy and I couldn't paint the pieces fast enough so I took in more painters and at its busiest I had 7 people making over old furniture. I had an amazing funny Irish man who used to source furniture for me. He'd stack it high on the roof of his car and bring it over for me. He truly was a sight to behold! He found the most fabulous pieces including church pews, travelling trunks and gentlemen's wardrobes. We'd stack it up in my little workshop at the back of my shop and I paint it piece by piece. It got to the point when people knew what day he was coming and would be waiting for him to arrive. They'd follow him in pick and pay for what they wanted there and then ready for me to paint. I remember one crazy busy day my shop was full in the morning but by late afternoon it was empty as I'd sold every single piece of furniture! They were happy times but the physical work was demanding and exhausting! I used to shut my shop on a Saturday night and go straight to the Turkish restaurant next door, where they would have my table waiting with my favourite glass of wine ready. A shop is so different from the virtual world we have now. There's only so many people you can squeeze into a shop no matter how hard you try!

I was passionate about Shabby Chic but I was also passionate about chocolate! Then one day whilst day dreaming my mind went ping, and another lightbulb moment was born! (I truly believe daydreaming gets your creative thoughts flowing!) I decided to combine my two passions and excitedly set about making plans and doing research. A few months later I opened 'Shabby Chocolat' a Rococo style Chocolate shop on the 1st floor of my furniture shop. It worked so well and looked stunning! I had armoires stocked with the most delicious chocolates. I also went to Paris to visit Salon du Chocolat to find some of the best chocolates I possibly could. I had a beautiful range made with rococo images of Marie Antoinette, Doves, Cherubs and crowns on them. I even got a tweet on Social Media from Joanna Harris who wrote the book Chocolate! I loved both my shops with a passion. Then came the dreaded floods of 2012 which in one day ruined a lot of the businesses in town. It wiped out a lot of trade in my shop and it was about 9 months before people started coming back. I remember being heartbroken how easily all your hard work could be wiped out by a single act of nature. I stayed on for another year but with constant threats of more floods I called it a day. Three months later there came the worst flood ever that would have completely wiped me out had I stayed. Upsetting as it was I'd made the right decision. Business in the real world has so many trials and problems to conquer and it's not the easiest of journeys. What to do next?

I didn't have to wait long as I was introduced to the revolution of Network Marketing! Sitting in the comfort of your own home making money from your sofa. What's not to like! No overheads, no stockpiling, no limit on how many customers you could have! I fell in love with the virtual world and all the different business opportunities it offered! My feet were itching again so not being restricted by a shop and being able to work from anywhere I spent some time travelling to my favourite spots in France and Europe. How amazing is the freedom you have working in the virtual world! Whilst in France I found the most amazing Crystal stall on the Cour Salaya market in Nice. I'd always been fascinated by Crystals since my holistic therapy days and had also learnt about other Universal Magic subjects such as Law of Attraction, Angels and Moonology to name a few but my favourite by far was Numerology. I just got it and understood it was truly the language of the universe. I'm also gifted intuitively and have always loved helping others with their own gifts and skills, especially within business. I started to see a new wave of women stepping forward. Women with a true entrepreneurial spirit.

I began doing one or two Numerology readings to help my clients them see their true selves. I realised there was a call for what I was doing so I put just one single post on Facebook asking if anyone would be interested in joining a group if I were to start one. I was blown away by the response and so Sassy

Soulpreneurs was born! I love my group. There are all sorts of inspirational women from all walks of life and different businesses but all with an awareness of the spiritual business wave we are entering. What has happened in the short space of time since launching is incredible. I share my knowledge of all my Universal Magic skills. I have connected with truly talented women and I now have worldwide clients who I read and prepare charts and forecasts for. I help empower women within my group to step into their own power and create their own success using their skills combined with Universal Magic. I use my intuition to spot upcoming niche businesses and have helped women to launch new spiritual wave businesses that weren't even in existence last year or even six months ago. There are so many on the horizon. We are heading into even more exciting times for virtual entrepreneurs. I also teach my skills through courses and help to inspire women in other groups too as a speaker.

I have been invited as a guest speaker at an event by two of the most amazing women leading at the front of this new empowerment industry. I've been nominated for a business award and featured in this book! I'm so grateful and blessed to be doing what I do. I could so easily have adopted a 'no hope' mindset from other people's views when first becoming a single mum. But let me tell you, the only view that matters is your own. So make it a good and empowered one. I could have given up after selling my clinic and put it down to ill health. But I made investments into my health and looked after myself and didn't use it as an excuse. I could have thrown the towel in and given up on being a business woman after the floods in Hebden Bridge. But I decided to come back even stronger and looked for new opportunities. Which as it happened has been the best ones yet! We have a whole new world of online Entrepreneurship opening up to us and we are only just at the tip of the iceberg! I truly believe there has been no better time for business than now! And there is so much more coming. But don't just sit back and expect it to happen, you have to put the work in! Even the Manifesters work at their craft!

Within the next two years I know there will be women becoming millionaires through the virtual world of social media. This new world is incredible. And it's there for everyone, with room for everyone. It doesn't matter where you're from, what your story is, if you have even a little spark of wanting to be successful, fan that flame! Believe in yourself and shine bright. This new wave of women entrepreneurs are all about lifting each other up! The thing is with success it's truly up to you if you want it or not. Nobody else can do it for you. There will be plenty of people who can hold you back. Even friends and family sometimes but that's mainly through fear. And don't fall into the trap of listening to the 'broke, but still the expert' sofa surfers! Surround yourself with the right kind of like-minded people. Not the negative Nelly's who just want to drag you down. Read, watch and soak up as much self-development as you possibly can. Every day we have is a learning day. It's important to have a positive money mindset and have a good relationship with money. Don't be afraid of it! Money is just an energy and it has to flow like a tide in and out. Don't be afraid to fail. Years ago failure in business could lead you in thousands of pounds in debt as you not only be left with stock but overheads and utility bills to pay too. With most virtual businesses this is now no longer the case. Most successful people were unsuccessful people first! Don't be afraid to take risks. And don't worry about what people think if your ideas are a bit 'wacky' 'woo' or 'out there!' They are usually the ones to succeed! But most of all don't be afraid of success either. Subconsciously this holds a lot of people back as their inner ego is scared of change. Working on your self-development and self-love can help resolve this problem. Meditation is a great way to get your mindset off to a good start. Do the daydreaming. Stretch your imagination. But most importantly spread your wings, take inspired action and shine your own brilliant light. Because believe me with the right mindset and input of work you can truly have the most amazing success you've ever dreamed of. So just go for it!

# 4. HANNAH

When I look back on my journey to my 46th year I feel mixed emotions; blessed to be alive, grateful for a second chance and joy that I get to share my life with beautiful people, my children and my partner. It could have been very different.

On the 5th December 2001 I was working in a supermarket on their customer services desk, it's what I'm good at, helping people. A thief had exited the store and I'd alerted the relevant authorities to deal with it. Myself and another manager had gone out of two different doors to see where he had gone. Next thing I know a car is being driven towards me at high speed, spun me round as my hand caught on the wing mirror and I fell to the floor crushing my foot under the back wheel. I knew instantly that I'd seriously broken my foot. As I lay there in agony, people rushing over to me, I knew I was lucky to be alive….it could have been a very different story if I'd been stood even 1 foot to the right. In hospital I was told it looked like a severe sprain, I knew otherwise and after an X-ray it was determined I'd broken 3 metatarsals, would need a walking cast for 10 weeks and then be back to normal. With a 20 month old and a 4 month old this was NOT going to be fun. It was nearly Xmas, we had to get lots of help, we hired a nanny! Two days later I had to return to hospital to have a more suitable cast put on. 3 hours of waiting and I asked why I had to wait so long. I was told a doctor needed to see me. The doctor came in and said, "This is a very serious injury, you've broken lots of bones in your foot and dislocated your ankle, we need to do surgery when the swelling has gone down to fix it. You may never walk again. If after the surgery we get you walking again the likelihood is that you'll have a limp and need a stick forever!" I just said, "You are joking aren't you?" His face said it all. How could they go from telling me I'd broken a few bones, would be 10 weeks in plaster to needing surgery and I may never walk again? I couldn't believe what I was hearing. I had young children, I needed to be fit for them. I had a life to lead. This was not an option for me. I remember that evening seeing a lad walking down the corridor on crutches, with only one leg, his foot cut off from the ankle. I decided there and then that that wasn't going to be me. I had to get walking again.

At this time I wondered why this had happened to me, I knew it had to have happened for a reason though! I decided to do everything the doctors told me, I have a strong will and will usually do things my own way but I knew I had to listen to them and the physio team. Every day I had to point, flex, twist my foot to keep the muscles working, as they'd pinned it all internally and I had a walking cast that I could put on when I went out. I did my exercises religiously, every 10-15 minutes throughout the day. The worst point was when I needed the toilet, just getting up to go upstairs meant all the blood rushed to my foot and left it throbbing and in pain but I had to carry on regardless. I never cried during this time, I figured if I started I might not stop and I knew I had to be positive in order to recover. That's been the key to a lot of my life I think, knowing that a positive attitude, even through adversity, will get you through the situation quicker. 3 months after the accident I had the pins removed and I had to learn to walk again, little by little with physio. The timeline they gave me was about 6 months to "walking", whatever that would look like. After 2 months I decided to sign myself out of physio because it was a waste of their time and resources. The team weren't happy about this but I asked them to watch what I could do. As I walked along the beam, stood completely still on the wobble board on my "bad" leg (which was actually now my good leg), and hopped along the floor on one leg they could see I was totally fine and not in need of any further help. I could walk. They said it was down to my positive mental attitude that this was possible as they didn't think it was. I left and picked up my life and carried on as normal.

A few months down the line my husband and I started to experience financial difficulties as we had had to pay for a nanny during this time, solicitors fees had caused a huge dent in our nonexistent savings (ok overdraft if you will!) and the pressure was starting to build. I wasn't happy in the area we lived and we moved with our children to a lovely leafy village with a traditional school and we started creating new friendships. My husband didn't like this move, it took him away (only by 10 minutes) from his family business, he left for work in the dark, came home in the dark, he was depressed but didn't really know it. The cracks started to appear in our relationship. We did some home improvements, bought some lovely things for our house but those things didn't make us happy. I made myself busy in the evenings, doing parties with my business selling jewellery and accessories in people's homes, so that I could get out. I made lots of acquaintances, lots of friends but I was always feeling left out, lonely, isolated. My drinking started to get worse. I had always had a problem with drink ever since I was about 17 when I would get very drunk at school parties and be ill. I didn't suddenly become a "drunk", it crept up on me, quietly throughout the years of unhappiness. The bottle became my friend, it became my comfort, the thing I could talk to. I would do parties and come home, open a bottle of wine and say…I'm just having one before bed….and before I knew it would be 5 o'clock in the morning, the TV and the lights would be on, I'd be sat on the sofa with an empty bottle of wine wondering where I was. I'd creep up to bed and hope I wouldn't wake him before he'd get up at 6 or 7 and go to work. Because I worked for myself I didn't have to be anywhere on time for anyone else. This only made it easier for me to drink and not feel the consequences. The children went to school in the village and they walked themselves to school by this point. It was easy for me, too convenient. Don't get me wrong, it wasn't like this all the time, but quite a lot of the time. When we went out my drinking would escalate and I'd be the "life and soul" of the party, being outrageous, flirting and being quite obnoxious and opinionated at times too. My ego definitely got in the way at times. I was always out to have a good time though. After a few more years of unhappy times I finally made the decision to leave. It was hard, it had been building for years. I suffered lots of verbal abuse by my ex, he never realised it, stating it was always sarcasm and "just a joke" but when you've been told "I could see your batwings flapping about" when you've just conducted an 80 strong choir for the first time it really does start to become anything but a joke! Especially when I'm only 5ft tall and size 8! Yeah right! How to knock the stuffing out of a tiny person who doesn't have much stuffing to start with!

The decision was made, we separated in the August of 2010, we sold our house and moved out November 2010. I suddenly found myself on my own with the children in a rented house in an area I didn't want to live in, with a travel to school and back every day. Stress levels were high. My drinking got worse. My finances suffered, my business too. I kept up the brave face though and ploughed on, knowing that life would get better. I met my current partner on December 18th 2010, the day most of England got covered by snow, online. I saw his face and knew him, we started dating. That Christmas was the worst one ever, my last one drinking. I went to my sisters for the day (my children were with their dad) and by 5pm I was brought home and put to bed because I was so drunk. I spent Boxing Day alone, waiting for my partner to come and see me. I stayed sober all that day, knowing I needed to make the most of the time I had with him. It was new and exciting but I was continuing my old ways of behaviour and had a few other "relationships" on the go. My life was crazy, I couldn't tell whether I was coming or going. I was smoking, drinking, sending people weird messages, behaving NOT how a 39 year old mum should be behaving. My new chap started to notice my drinking and questioned it a few times, whether I was an alcoholic. I denied it every time, but deep down had a feeling that something wasn't right. When I had been with my husband I thought I drank to annoy him. He wasn't around anymore and my drinking was getting worse. The days when I wouldn't see my chap I would be drinking all afternoon and evening, ping ponging around the house after 1-2 bottles of wine. I would stagger upstairs in the early hours of the morning and hope the kids would be fine in the morning getting themselves to school! On the days when I was scheduled to see him I would be tetchy, jumpy, nervous but knowing that I was ok because tomorrow would be another day and I could drink again. I actually started to enjoy our time together when I wasn't drinking. Life was confusing, up and down, an emotionrollercoaster. The situation with my ex was hard too, changes in routine for children, our divorce getting sorted, so much going on. I always tried to remain positive though, knowing it would all be ok one day. I had seen other friends go through stuff like this so I figured I would too.

On the evening of the 6th July 2011 everything changed. I hit rock bottom, when I finally realised I was an alcoholic, I had lost the man who finally "got me" and I knew I couldn't risk losing anymore. The following morning when I woke up I messaged my youngest sister saying "I need help, can you get here?" She messaged straight back, "I'll be there in 20 minutes". She found me crying at the bottom of the stairs asking God for help. I'm not an overly religious person but I know my higher power was working with me that day. Her partner at the time was in AA so she called him and he took me to my first meeting that night. To this day I haven't touched a drop of alcohol. I feel fortunate, one of the lucky ones who just gets it first time. The reality of it is I don't want to do day one ever again because it was shocking. If I took a drink now I'd have to start again and that is not an option for me. People ask me if I'll have a drink one day, I don't know the answer to that, I just know that it's just for today, tomorrow is another day and is only given to us when we sleep and wake up the next day.

I wake up with gratitude now that I have been given another day to experience life and all it has to offer. There have been times I've been tempted but I just play the video in my head forward about 4 hours and see the state I'd be in and that's enough to stop me. When my partner asked me to marry him the first thing I thought of is I won't be able to sip champagne anymore. Elderflower is a great alternative though! Those first few months whizzed by, I had my 40th 2 months after coming into AA. I remember every single thing about it, especially my Dad getting merry and playing chopsticks as drums on the table whilst we were karaoke singing in the Chinese restaurant! Throughout this last 6 years since I stopped drinking life has obviously changed for me. I've stayed sober, helped other people in AA, been of service too. Taking the position of secretary at the beginners meeting was important for me, it kept me sober too when my dear friend decided to depart this earth….because it could have been a very different story otherwise. I've always tried to remain positive when things go wrong, or get tough, or my partner and I would have fall outs or disputes. I would know that it was just a passing phase and that things would be ok if I stayed sober. 2 years after starting that journey I found a new business, a networking business and it has been the thing that has pushed me on in personal development alongside AA. Ironically they both have the same principles….go to meetings, help other people and you'll be successful along with those people. It's the same in my business as it is for AA.

My personal and business lives have begun to intertwine and I do now have some people in my business who've sought help for addictions and mental issues too. My business has provided me with lots of personal development books and audio CDs which I listen to in my car, my car university as I call it. Mindset is the biggest thing I've had to work on during this time because life throws all sorts of mud at us during our time here on earth. We let people, places and things affect us when all we can control are our own actions, our own thoughts. We don't have to let other people's actions and words affect us, but they do and it's this state of mind that stops us progressing and becoming the best version of ourselves, so we have to work on it. I have had to learn that sometimes people say no to us, they don't want to hear what we have to say. It's not personal, it's just business. I've learnt that thinking positively really does make all the difference to the outcome of one's actions.

If you think you can't do something you're right, if you think you can do something you're right. The mind is a very powerful thing and is either an asset or a liability to us, in fact everything we do is! The food we eat, the books we read, the TV we watch, the company we keep, the job we have, the relationship we're in, it's all either an asset or a liability to ourselves. I've learnt that no matter what is occurring in my life it is all part of a great journey, to be experienced like weaving through a maze, one entry stops, another opens, another path is blocked so you try
another one, but ultimately we all reach the end having been on a journey. It's what we do on that journey that counts. During these last few years I've reignited my passion for music. I now teach piano to children and adults, and play for old people in old people's homes and do weddings and parties. When my accident happened the nanny who looked after us became a good

friend, she introduced me to the Oxford Gospel Choir and I sang with them for about 2-3 years before my ex and I split up.

When my friend died I found it very hard to sing and so left. Recently I was feeling discontented as I wasn't doing any music for myself so I decided to go back to choir. I found my voice again and have taken part in TV recordings and concerts and performed some solos with the choir. What I realised recently was that my accident brought me my friend who introduced me to choir, where I found the courage through singing to leave my ex and that my accident had indeed happened for a reason, to help me help others, to realise I needed help myself too and to start my journey into alcoholic recovery, to accept that I'm a musician who has a gift to share with the world and to live my life with purpose and passion. It's something I now help others to do, through coaching or business or simply play-ing the piano. The exciting thing for me is….I wonder what the next 50 years will bring?

# 5. FILI

For as long as I can remember, I have ALWAYS been "that girl". The one that would sit right up in the front of the class alone, 'sociable' yet alone. The one that was expected to get good grades, head into University, get a good career and then start a family. But my story unfolded very differently, in fact, it had unfolded almost in reverse. I am the eldest of three daughters from a very traditional Samoan family. My parents migrated from our motherland in 1990 to New Zealand in the hopes of a better life for themselves and the family they were going to have. My parents sacrificed everything to give my sisters and I the life they did not have back home in Samoa. Some would argue that we were spoilt, though our Father made sure that we knew our limits. We grew up in a very religious and cultural environment where from a very early age- Christianity, Religion, Hard work and Family were paramount values that were instilled in my sisters and I. The norm we lived was one of a working family with Mum attending evening business classes after her full-time job and then coming home to us. So, it was only fitting for me to have followed that normalised status quo of- going to school, getting into university and attaining a degree to find a career. My sisters and I attended our local schools and I was the very first grandchild on both sides of my family to achieve University entrance to attend one of the top Universities in New Zealand. My first year at University was where life changed DRAMATICALLY. The girl with good grades, who was the first out of both sides of her family to get into University fell pregnant. Life was beginning to unravel in "reverse" literally.

My husband and I got married six months after dating and our daughter arrived in June of 2012. The challenges we faced as a young couple felt as though they were magnified when we became parents. When it was just my husband and I, things were okay financially – we managed. Then two mouths turned into three mouths and things began to get a little difficult. We felt as though we couldn't breathe and were so thankful to have still been (are still) living with my parents. I saw my husband wake up in the early hours of the morning to head off to work and our daughter wouldn't see him until later in the evening. I saw my daughter going through the exact same reality that I lived at her age. My parents worked long hours to be able to provide my sisters and I a comfortable life. I had come to realise that if my husband were to come home one day and proceed to tell me that he did not have a job or if he were to fall ill and couldn't work – we would not have a backup plan in place, yet we had a little girl depending on us. It was here that I started to look for other ways to help supplement my husbands' income. I realised that I also wanted to bring the most important people home, my husband and parents. I started actively looking for other avenues to earn an income for my family whilst juggling full-time studies. I came across a network marketing company, however, my prior assumptions about network marketing was that it was a "pyramid scheme". HECK, I didn't even know what a pyramid scheme was. "Society" normalised looking elsewhere to earn an extra income beside the 9 to 5 as some sort of "get-rich-quick-scheme" that was illegal. I had no clue that when I had joined the first company, that what I was in fact signing up to was a network marketing based company. Prior to the company we are partnered with currently, we were with a health and beauty based company. Absolutely loved the concept and personal growth however, it was far from an "easy" journey. This company we were previously partnered with, required us to push through state-of-the-art health and beauty products that helped many customers with issues they faced. Absolutely loved the products but the longer we stayed in business, the more difficult it was financially for us to maintain business. The longer we stayed in, the more political it had gotten and the more stress and strain it had caused for the important relationships in my life. It was during my time with this first company that I came across the amazing Leona Burton – courtesy of our mutual friend and queen of mindset – Emma Privilege. I had approached Leona about something and before I knew it I was agreeing to being mentored and coached by her. The best thing to have happened to me on my journey as a business Mumma. For about three months, Leona called me once a week to discuss how things were going with business. Reflecting back on my journey with that first company I realised the many struggles we had faced were in fact moments of growth and served as a stepping stone to the greater and brighter things in my life.

A massive struggle we endured in our first business venture was trying to "maintain points" to get paid a minimum commission. I understood going into this that we were offering people hope by pinpointing the issues they had and offering a solution. What I had later come to realise was that I was now merely 'selling' products to family and friends that were not necessarily a necessity for them but they were purchasing these as a courtesy to me. It was there that I realised that I did not want to keep doing that to them.

During this time came the strain on the marriage – I'm sure I am not the only business mama and wife that has lived through this struggle. I had this dream that we would be able to build this business together but I was inflicting upon him all these expectations that did not once at all align with what he wanted out of life. I was being selfish but I was so blinded by 'what could be' that I did not stand to see what I could do to serve my husband as his partner and wife and to help him achieve the goals he had set out for himself. It was more about maintaining a façade that we were this "power-couple" when in all reality we were drowning – physically and emotionally. The final major straw behind stepping away from the first business was the fact that we lost our passion to serve and help people. You see, the reason I felt so strongly about what I was doing was because I was prophesied over and it was made certain that what I was doing I was "meant" to do. The platform that I would be able to build for myself, I would be able to use to help other women in their life journey. The platform provided to me through network marketing would allow me to serve and grow in my faith as a Christian. However, the passion to serving others was rapidly dwindling when it was as though we were just counting down the days of the months and oblivious to the fact that we were wasting time. It became about, 'month's end' and 'start of the month' that nothing in between seemed to matter. It literally felt as though we opened our eyes at the beginning of each month, blink and were scrambling during the last couple of days of the month to find money to try and maintain points to get paid. A contributing factor to this struggle of trying to get "paid" was the politics I felt with the new up line I had acquired. She wore her heart on her sleeve but at times I felt as though my interests never mattered. It almost felt as though I was being "bossed" rather than "coached and mentored". When I knew I had to step away from this business, I literally felt as though my life was ending. This business became what I lived and breathed and shared on social media for the past year of my life. It had become a part of me. It had to have been the hardest decision I ever had to make. I remember messaging my up lines letting them know with tears rolling down my face. I remember how heavy my heart felt but I knew in my gut it was the right decision for my family and I at the time. The feelings of feeling like a failure became almost unbearable but again the amazing Leona Burton struck again. What I remember from the conversations we had prior to my official decision was along the lines of, "No-one cares if you have stopped or not. Who cares what people think. Are they paying your bills?" This was the very first time where I thought, "OMG – its' okay to stop doing things if it is for the betterment of my future. Stuff the status quo". For many years I have always been one to be very hard on myself. I would set these really high expectations of myself that I felt as though it was never okay to "fail" or stop doing something that was causing more harm than good to me. I learnt a really important lesson here, "DO NOT GIVE A 2PIECES ABOUT WHAT ANYONE ELSE THINKS. DO WHAT IS BEST FOR YOU AND YOUR FAMILY". Now for those who know me personally, I have this talent of really placing the entire planet on my shoulder and caring about the irrelevant opinions of others. Glad to FINALLY say that I have learnt my lesson. Although this was a difficult journey to have walked through I am absolutely thankful because from each struggle, there was a silver lining. I realised that my journey with this first company was in-fact a stepping stone to greater things.

Some key lessons that I took away from being a part of this first company was that, the passion to serve should never dwindle. When the passion is continuously ignited within you daily, that is when it becomes a calling. I realised that the politics that I had been facing of "up line politics" blocked my vision of the greater picture but what emerged was the realisation of exactly the type of up line I wanted to be for others. My journey highlighted many character building moments of learning patience and respect with and for my husband. He had been an amazing support from the very beginning, but it was when I had placed all these expectations upon him …. this was where issues therein emerged. I had come to realise that my life companion was supporting me and the vision I had for my life and family, but the expectations placed upon him were becoming a burden. I am truly grateful, reflecting back on my journey because it has taught me to respect and be patient with not only my husband but those whom I come into business with. The realisation that this journey with our first ever network marketing company, served as a stepping stone to greater things- is what I have come to vividly believe now that I have found a vehicle that I have been able to utilise and capitalise upon.

"Cous, lets catch up – I really want to show you some information", the words that literally changed the course of our lives in the last 32 days. Of-course starting a new business wasn't really something that my husband and I had in mind especially with the struggles we faced with the first business venture. However, one of my good friends nudged me to go with an open heart and mind because she knew first-hand the struggles we had been facing. We first jumped on to a zoom conference call where we were exposed to the information and at first it was an "ahem" moment. We were then invited to a Saturday Regional Training Event and obviously I dragged my husband along with me. We were both still quite reluctant to go but we turned up anyway. Long story short, they start playing this DVD showing how we could generate an income from the bills we already pay and literally it clicked for us. Not only the concept but the energy and vibe of the leaders in the room really drew us in. We FINALLY saw a way that we could bring home the most important people to us. We signed up as Independent Business Owners the next day and our lives have never been the same. My husband- the stone mason, I have come to realise is an absolute undercover recruiting machine. This man has literally come out of his shell. He takes our leadership trainings and is hands-on involved with this business that I didn't even need to ask him if we were in. He responded after our very first exposure, "When are we doing this thing. LET'S DO THIS". It has definitely been a breath of fresh air to be able to build this business with my life companion. Of course, there are days where we want to throttle one another (with hugs), but what we have found is my strengths are his weaknesses and vice versa. This has allowed us to grow as individuals and also gel as a dynamic duo to build different aspects of the same business. It FINALLY feels good to be able to connect with one another on different levels apart from the emotional connection as husband and wife. It is and has been a blessing to be able to grow together. For any other business mamas out there who are struggling with a spouse who is yet to grasp the vision you see (with whatever business you may be running), don't force it. Don't let a disagreement regarding being business partners to be a burden on the both of you. If it is meant to happen...trust me, it will happen.

Smashing through comfort zones and taking the family with me is something that I am truly thankful to have been able to foster. I realised that all that needed to happen to change the legacies that we leave our children was to step out in faith and do something different. We absolutely love that we have my mother slaying the business as one of our top producing business partners, my brother and sister in-law also saw a way to fulfil their dreams and make them a reality and we have crossed paths with other young parents and families inspired to take action for a better life for themselves. It is here that I realised that I am finally "Home". I am so privileged and humbled to be mentored and coached by one of the best in the company and even more so because of the system that this business utilises. The business dynamic is far different to the one we experienced with the first business venture and we are thankful for that experience because it has allowed us to appreciate the blessing of an amazing business vehicle we are now a part of. I have been able to coach the team and lead and inspire which is what I have always felt my calling to be. It has been an absolute blessing to have finally found a vehicle in the network marketing industry that is allowing me to impact lives and to make a difference. Network marketing has allowed me to grow. This industry has allowed me to smash through my comfort zone, it has allowed me to value my mindset and personal growth. Network marketing has changed my life in so many positive ways. I attribute the changes in my life to this industry that so many people look down upon. What people don't realise is that network marketing essentially is an industry built on personal growth and development. It is a way for individuals to better themselves and their lives through growth. We are going to cross paths with those who are not fully able to appreciate or comprehend the value that network marketing has as an industry and that's okay. I'm here to let you know that it is totally okay to do something out of the normalised 9 to 5 if it means you are creating something for the betterment of your future.

The introvert, Samoan university student and stone mason achieved the unimaginable through crushing through comfort zones to create a security financial blanket around their family. We never once thought that we could build a business together. We never once thought our lives would work out to how it has unfolded. We never once thought that network marketing would be the answer to our struggles. If there is anyone out there who feels as though "they don't deserve much out of life" and that its okay to "settle", realise this as a mini reality check. We were not put on this Earth to settle. We were not put on this Earth to be mediocre. We were, we ARE destined for more. The drive to be great in life is what one should hold onto when attempting to do things out of the norm. Your reason WHY should help surpass the negativity that is bound to be present. There will be negativity present and may even be from your circle of love, but that should serve as a reminder to keep going. No-one said it was going to be easy but it will definitely be worth it. All these things paired together with a passion to live an abundant life and to help others do the same, will create the most unstoppable YOU. Step out in faith and write and own your life story. If the university student who fell pregnant in her teens, got married and graduated with an undergraduate degree after 6 years (meant to be three) and the stone mason who struggled through school and whom were both introverts - step out of their comfort zones to change legacies left behind and literally change the course of their family tree – then ANYONE can too. Just believe in you and fly.

# 6. KATIE H

I remember my daddy asking me what I was going to be when I was older. It was a Sunday morning and I was wedged in the middle of my parent's bed all warm and safe. My response was always "I'm going to sip tea and ride my horses around my grounds" Well I got the sipping tea bit right but after one stint at horse riding lessons it became clear that wouldn't be happening. "Can we try it again without the sound effects please Katie?" bellowed the riding instructor. Then she asked me to pick up the horse poo so I cried and had to be fetched early. Who would have thought back then that I would be a Psychic Medium reading for individuals worldwide.

My first memory of my gift was when I was three years old, my mom found me talking to the old lady that used to live in our house. I remember how kind she was to me her name was Lillian. She asked me to tell my mom to look after her beautiful roses in the garden and I remember my mom going pale when I passed on the message. I would talk about family members I had seen in dreams that had passed on, I would comment on people walking around whilst we were out and about only to be told nobody else could see them. It wasn't until I got to my early teens that I became upset by my gift, I had realised not everyone was like me, I was frightened to go to sleep. My parents spoke to the Vicar that lived next door and he had agreed to pop round and bless our house. My older brother always teased me and used to follow me around with a crucifix whilst laughing. He was told off and soon skulked away. The Vicar also advised my Mom to find someone that could help me develop my gift. Unfortunately at that time there wasn't the circle groups that there are now. However knowing that people believed me outside of the family was a huge weight lifted. The sad thing about growing older is you start to put barriers up, I was worried my gift wouldn't be socially accepted and I started to hide it. Obviously not very well as word got out at school and on a lunchtime and I started running a palm reading service, in a convent catholic school might I add. Can you imagine? In Year 11 career counsellors visited school and again I was told I needed a plan, where was my focus? The only thing I was sure about in life was that I was going to be a Mom, I absolutely LOVE children, the way they think, and the inappropriate things they say. I also knew I was meant for great things and had faith it would all be ok. This laid back approach to life caused great concern from my teachers. I had my first full time job at the age of 17, I had decided I wanted to go and work in an office, the basis of this was because I wanted to dress up. The day I walked into the interview a handsome guy opened the door for me and said "wow" I took one look at him and thought "I'm going to marry you one day" and as it happens I did. I didn't take the job seriously, I made friends, spent my entire monthly salary in one day every month and wrote Mr. H love notes using all the office stationery. I now know I was only meant to be there to meet my Mr. H. I then moved on and worked in a bank, I had to be serious and knuckle down as they were very strict and I was told the pensions and bonuses were great. I did not care, I felt bored, trapped and thought there is no way I'm working here for the next 30 years. However something amazing happened myself and Mr. H had just moved into a one bedroom apartment in the centre of town and we were pregnant with our first daughter. Sadly at the same time I lost my amazing Grandad, he was the most fantastic man and saw the potential in me. I was devastated he would never meet my baby or see me get married. However I now know our loved ones never really leave us.

On Christmas Eve 2003 I was in hospital ready to be induced with our first daughter, sadly things didn't go to plan and I suffered placenta abruption. All I remember is blood and severe pain, being rushed down to delivery suite whilst hearing carol songs in the background. The hospital managed to stabilise my blood loss and told me to rest until the contractions started. I looked around the room feeling relieved and calm only to see lots of spirits. There were nuns, casually dressed people all just sat there chatting away. I knew then I wasn't going to be ok and I prayed it would be me and not the baby. They had been sent to look after me or collect me I wasn't sure which. My gorgeous baby Jesus was born on Christmas day and was a picture of health, I on the other hand was dying. There was so much blood that a midwife slipped on it and had to go home. I woke up in intensive care and was just grateful I was alive. I made a vow to take my gift seriously as I was so grateful to have them all come and look after me. I started to research spiritual circles and made one of my friends from the bank come with me to one, it was weird they made us all dance round the rooms with scarves and I never went back. I looked into other groups but nothing felt right. I started to read for people in their houses and the feedback was amazing. I had to keep it quiet though as I didn't want to burn my bridges with my banking job. Then I fell pregnant with our second daughter and I remember travelling to read for people whilst heavily pregnant. Passing on messages from loved ones was an amazing feeling and I knew this was what I was meant to be doing but how could I grow? After our beautiful second daughter was born I was overwhelmed by how connected I was to our girls, I knew what they were thinking, what they needed and if they were poorly well in advance. I was so in tune with them they were calm, placid babies. They both ignited a desire in me to be successful I wanted to give them every opportunity I had whilst growing up. I wanted to be the best example to them and show them that dreaming about being a princess was fantastic and not having a plan was great too. I joined another spiritualist church and found this one was actually quite normal, every week we would work on opening up through meditation, how to connect with spirit in different ways and then pair up with different people each week. My connection to spirit was so strong that I would reel off a full reading and leave my partner dumbfounded. I was told a few times to stop "showing off" I wasn't showing off at all I just wanted to make sure I had passed on everything I had been told. I was desperate to try platform work (where you stand in front of an audience and connect to spirit) but I was always told no. They were completely right I had to learn to close off, protect myself, filter the information respectfully and break it down as it's not always given to you clearly. I was like a hyperactive toddler and I can see how I must have really annoyed them all. The circle group ended and I continued to read privately around my two babies and a full time job, it was no surprise I became exhausted and decided to concentrate on my job and the family and I took a break from spirit world. We then had another surprise we fell pregnant with our third daughter and I was delighted. We hadn't planned to have any more children but secretly I wanted six. I embraced the pregnancy and really enjoyed it and had made some new Mom friends at my daughter's school that all wanted readings. So there I was reading whilst heavily pregnant again, when I look back now I can see I was always brought back to my gift.

Our third baby was born and I knew exactly what time she would arrive, we were all in love and our family felt complete. Life was great and then five days after her birth I woke up in the night with the worst headache of my life and I was freezing cold. It was the hottest night of the year so I couldn't understand why I was shivering. I got rushed into hospital and was told I had septicaemia, I was so poorly I just wanted to sleep and be left. I found myself back in the same room in intensive care and I could see clouds right in front of me, I felt calm and peaceful until the machines started beeping and the nurse shouted "Katie what are you doing? Come back" I can honestly say at that time I thought I'm dying again and actually it's ok I feel very peaceful. It was a surreal experience. When you experience these surreal moments it really makes you put your life into perspective, I wasn't going to waste my time. I was grateful to be here and I was going to make something of myself. I began working as a PA in higher education and I actually enjoyed it, the academics were quirky like me and you were allowed to think freely. The academics would often say "Educate yourself Katie, you're wasted" but with three children and limited time this option was just not feasible. Instead I put everything into my job and it started to pay off I was well respected and learnt some new skills. Outside of work I joined a crystal circle to see if I could develop my psychic ability further, however with three young daughters and a full time job I couldn't attend every week. Sadly I started to become unwell with very strange symptoms, tummy swelling, and awful periods and really lethargic. I went back and forth to hospitals and my GP and couldn't get any answers. I started to become withdrawn and thought I was imaging these symptoms. I couldn't look after the girls' every day and had to rely on Mr. H and our parents. I had to take time out from my job and sadly over seven years lost many opportunities on the grounds of ill health. When I look back now these were amazing opportunities and I was genuinely devastated. I was still reading but only a few and through recommendations only. The Doctors decided I needed a hysterectomy and this was a HUGE decision for me as I always wanted more children. However I knew I had to proceed as my life was effectively on hold. I was worried my girls would think it was normal to have a mom constantly ill and in hospital. So I agreed to proceed and booked myself in for January 2015. My consultant was amazing and had we have met in different circumstances I think we would have been great friends. The few weeks leading up to the operation I think I temporarily lost the plot, I would cry for no reason and I was petrified I would die and Mr. H and the trio would be without me. On the day of the operation I wasn't too bad I had pulled myself together and decided to be brave, before they put me to sleep I begged all the theatre staff to keep me safe and a few of them hugged me. I will never forget their kindness. When I woke up I felt amazing, I think I was just grateful I had woken up. I decided then that was it I was going to change my whole life nothing was going to stop me I was a new women. Mr. H thought I was having a breakdown but I had never been so sure. It was then I decided to join the world of network marketing, everyone thought I was mad but to me it made perfect sense. I could work from home, around my girls and earn a fantastic income. Well that was the plan anyway. I needed to have flexible working as I couldn't take the disappointment of losing another job down to ill health. Even though the operation was a success, I was terrified it hadn't worked and all the symptoms would come back. Health really is wealth without it you have nothing. So I started building my empire and absolutely loved it, the training was phenomenal, there were people from all walks of life and from all over the world. They taught me how to brand myself, use social media for business, be a leader and most importantly work on myself. I met the most incredible people two of which are very special to me and I know we were meant to meet. Eighteen months later I decided the company I was with was quite saturated so I decided to partner with another company and in particular with a lady called Jo who I had huge respect for. I grew with this company very quickly and received promotion after promotion. I was back I felt like me again, I was living my dream.

However destiny had a different path for me as I kept being

asked if I was still reading. Then one day out of the blue I decided to contact a lady called Sarah Morgan, she had left the world of network marketing to become a manifesting coach and I felt compelled to talk to her. I started crying telling her I was frightened of failure even though I had been successful. I kept telling her something was missing but I didn't know what. Sarah advised I just keep doing what makes me happy and what will be will be, she was so right. I cannot thank her enough for the time she gave me that day. After a training call with my new mentor Jo, she mentioned she was off to have a psychic reading. I explained my ability and she said "Are you joking? You're a psychic?" She asked me to read for her over video chat and I said I would try, I had only ever read in person. The reading went really well and the connection was just as strong. Jo kindly mentioned to people about my gift and then I was flooded with requests. Jo made me realise just how strong my gift is and encouraged me to pursue it. For that and may other things I will always be very grateful to her. With every reading I was feeling more fulfilled and ready to take on whatever was going to come of this. The feedback I've received is amazing and I feel compelled to help more people. I have set up a Facebook group, launched a website and asked people to recommend if they were happy to do so. Sarah and I decided to work together at the Mind Body and Spirit event at the NEC Birmingham and we met some remarkable people. We have also held a joint online event where we combined the world of manifesting and spiritualism. Due to our success we have plans in place to launch an academy and host future events. Then I started receiving global reading requests and have been reading for people all over the world. I'm literally blown away. My future goals are to fill theatres and read on a grander scale, to travel all over the world and to write a book. I also want to help people develop psychic ability and really help people connect with themselves and discover what their sole purpose is. I'm very grateful for everything that's happened to me as it's lead me to where I was supposed to be. I'm even grateful for the near death experiences as without them I wouldn't appreciate how precious life really is. My trio are my biggest inspiration to see them proud of my achievements makes my heart swell. I know I will be able to offer them every opportunity in life and that is just priceless. For all you readers out there I just want to say be proud of where you are right now, it might not be where you want, but have faith your life is all mapped out for you. Sometimes we have to experience bad times to get to the good times. I believe there's no such thing as a bad decision, when I look back now I can see how all the different events and people in my life have been like a jigsaw puzzle, every piece was relevant and it all comes together in the end. Have faith and be confident that your guardian angels will look after you. Keep going, enjoy your journey and remember always be kind along the way.

# 7. HOLLIE

At aged 11 I answered the phone to a UK television company and was given the news that they had written me a character into their award winning children's TV show and my life was about to change. To most this would have been staggering, but to me it felt the natural next step in my journey and I was so excited.

I grew up in Newcastle Upon Tyne, an industrial city in the north east of England, in a working class home full of love. My Dad a welder who spent time working on oil rigs and my Mum who worked in a bank. No one in my family came from the entertainment industry and yet here I was suddenly beginning my dream job and bringing in money at only 11 years old. I had no idea how this would change the course of my life. I grew up on TV, playing the part of Emma Miller, a popular character on UK children's drama, Byker Grove, which at the time was watched by millions. I played that part for 7 years and then left to pursue a singing career. My character on the show had began a singing career and like life imitating art, I had been approached by Sony and had been secretly recording material, ready for leaving the show.

As a singer I did the rounds of TV shows such as MTV, Disney, Nickelodeon and iconic UK music show, Top Of The Pops. I travelled the UK appearing at clubs and on radio shows, springing up in every major newspaper and magazine in the UK.

Life seemed easy.

The music industry was changing though and with the rise of Music talent shows, such as Pop Idol, record labels no longer nurtured their talent, it was top ten or you were out. My first single bounced in at 32 in the UK charts and I took a call to say "thanks, it's been great working with you and good luck."

What? Suddenly I realised that things don't always go to plan. I hadn't ever considered this before. Life had seemed simple and this was a huge blow, but also the best lesson I could ever have had.

Over the next year I was back to basics, I was auditioning for TV shows and films and travelling from Newcastle to London every week on a train. It was costing me a fortune and the money I had saved from my time in Byker grove was being whittled down. I worked two jobs, one in a cafe and one at a museum, but was narrowly missing major roles every week. So I decided I need to go to drama school and move to London. After auditioning for the best drama schools in the country I was offered a place at the prestigious East 15 Acting School.

At drama school I realised that if I wanted to act I had to make money. Acting can be an expensive business and I have never been a poor actor. But being at drama school, there was little room to work and I started my first steps into entrepreneurship. I printed off flyers and walked my local area handing them out and pushing them through peoples doors. I offered myself up as a cleaner , babysitter and admin help. I cleaned houses, I worked at a psychologists house, typing for him in his shed office as he dictated the book he was writing (a job my Dad begged me to stop doing!) and I worked as a waitress in a strip club.I wanted to live and I wanted to know that I wasn't scared to do whatever it took to have a nice life. During the holidays of drama school I learnt about promotional modelling and I found a new way to work around what I really wanted to do. This meant I spent my weekends giving out chocolate bars, dressed as a yoghurt, smiling in cocktail dresses at events and selling alcohol at prestigious parties. I enjoyed this way of working, it was good fun, made me very good money and developed my confidence.

I was still auditioning whilst being at drama school (although this was definitely not allowed) and two weeks before finishing my first year I left. I had been offered a major role in one of the most popular TV shows in the UK, at the time, Waterloo Road. It was worth the risk and I packed a bag and headed to Manchester, back in the north of England.

After finishing Waterloo Road I bounced around from TV show, to film roles and even worked as a CBEEBIES (under 5's) radio presenter. I worked fairly consistently and although I was still doing promotional work i made the bulk of my money from acting and modelling. Alongside acting and entertainment work I was always coming up with ways to make money, that worked around auditions and acting and when I met my husband, Ross he taught me how to make 'me' into a business and I began taking my brand seriously.

Just a few of the business ventures I have embarked on (not all successfully), teaching an adult acting class, Imapregnantmodel.com (used during both pregnancies), The Headshot Doctor (an actors headshot company), teaching people confidence techniques 1:1, getting girls selling shots in bars across Essex and helping to launch a reality TV show.

As an actor I had always worked on my mindset, having to take rejection after rejection, regardless of your success, can take its toll on anyone and so I was heavily into self-development.

At 26 I became a mum for the first time to baby Brooke, a

premature baby, born 6 weeks too early and two years later my second daughter, Texas came into the world. By then I had several revenue streams; acting, teaching, speaking, writing, modelling and working with brands and our lives as a family were pretty great. Then in 2014 we took the news that everyone dreads.

"I'm sorry Mr. Blair, but you have a brain tumour. We will do what we can but if we cannot help we will just make you comfortable" the words rang in my ears and I felt like I was being sucked into the floor. Suddenly our lives took a very different turn. I phoned my agent. I had been booked for a film and was to begin filming the next week. Not now. I told her I didn't want to work and I focused on my family.

Brain surgeries, chemotherapy, radiotherapy followed, doctor's appointments, injections, pills and a shift in roles for us as a couple. Our lives were changed. I changed. I can vividly remember coming home from the hospital, on my own for perhaps the first time since we had Ben told that it was grade 4, rare and he had 50/50 chance of surviving 5 years. I sat on my kitchen floor and I sobbed. I cried for what felt like forever, the really ugly cries and then suddenly I had more clarity than I had ever had in my life. I realised in that moment that if I wanted to be happy, it was me that was going to make that happen and I decided that I would do 'whatever it took' to get me and my family through this period in our lives.

Then I took stock, I looked at what I wanted for my life and I brought my work closer to home. I initially started a network marketing company, built a successful team and made a very decent amount of money around my family, but after a time I realised that this way of working didn't work for me. Although I have huge respect and love for those that work within this industry and it certainly taught me a lot, I began to feel that it was shifting into something that resembled a job and that doesn't suit someone like me. I did however learn some very valuable business lesson, more about self-development and spoke at huge events, which increased my confidence as a speaker. What I realised most thought was that I only really enjoyed coaching people and building people's belief in themselves. that side of network marketing I adore and so i knew that was something I wanted to still focus on.

So I stopped and took stock again. What did I want? Where was I not quite getting it right? I spent about 3 months in a very low period of my life, that I now see as my transitional time. During this time of stopping I realised that my love of self-development, entrepreneurship and people had already combined to build my own personal brand and I just had to work more on that.

I hired a personal business coach and I got to work. This fabulous lady blew some life back into me and reminded me of who I am. During this period in my life my husband was having more regular seizures brought on by the brain cancer, I had a young family and my sisters partner had been diagnosed with leukaemia. I had started to doubt myself and shape myself into a box that wasn't me. In working with this coach I realised that who I am and all the chaos that brings with it, it just great. I stopped trying to fit into the mold of what I thought a business woman was supposed to look like and unleashed my 'f*ck it!'. I invested heavily in myself so that I could be the best for others. I got back to doing things I love. I began writing, reading and learning again and filling my time with positivity. I began learning about the online marketing world and developing business and mindset courses people could buy and developed a revenue stream that meant once I had done the work I could earn even in my sleep, this excited me.

My husband's health was largely pretty good at this time and although the cancer was always in the background, we lived a happy life. My coaching practice soared and I was also asked to become a paid vlogger for Channel Mum, an ITV affiliate and fantastic network of women. I was nominated for awards for my YouTube channel, Holly Matthews online, where I talk about my life and positive mindset and I had began to have brands contacting me to work with me. I became a high pro-file supporter of The Brain Tumour Charity and talked openly about the realities of our life.

I launched my first major online self-development course, with a psychologist friend of mine Caroline Hardwick called The Bossing it! Academy. Bossing it! is a law of attraction course, for those that like straight talking self-development and quickly gained some big exposure. We had celebrities, influencers and household names through our virtual doors and were featured on the BBC and in The Daily Mirror.

Then in July 2017 my husband died. It felt sudden. We had spent a wonderful holiday in Turks and Caicos and on our return Ross had a seizure and began to deteriorate. It was quick, it was brutal and I spent a month living in a hospice with him. Everyone rallied round, the support was incredible. I talked openly about what was going on and drew strength from the knowledge my authentic living could help others live their truth too. In my time in the hospice I mediated daily, I focused on gratitude, I worked on my business, wrote, even selling online products from his bedside. I also helped raise over £11,000 for the hospice that gave my husband such a dignified end of life.

I am nearly 5 months on from his death as I write this and although the pain is deep, there are also beautiful things hap-pening in mine and my families life too. During my time in the hospice I had been seeking out those that had walked the path in front of me. People who had gone through tough stuff but soared. I didn't want to see people who are a wreck, I wanted to see positivity, strength and hope. Society often wants us to squeeze into a box and when it comes to grief and loss we expect a certain decorum and we want people to play the grieving widower. I am not a victim and knowing I was losing my best friend I sat one morning and meditated on finding other that could guide me. I promised myself I would block out those that made me feel bad and those that played victim and I would find those souls who were thriving no matter what. 30 minutes after that meditation I found myself in a group chat on Facebook being introduced to a lady who wanted to put me in a book about entrepreneurial women and feature in me on Forbes as women to look out for in 2018! Not only that but this woman is incredible and shared with me that she too had been in a hospice, with her dying son and had been in the same place I was in then. That encounter wasn't chance, it wasn't magic either, it was me focusing my brain on what I wanted and seeking that out, bringing that to my reality. That lady told me she wanted to give me light at the end of the tunnel and it really was.

Since Ross died, I have allowed myself to be. If I want to cry I cry, if I want to laugh I laugh and it's all OK. I have spent my last few months developing my newest online self-development course, The Happy Me Project. This is 21 days of positivity, audios, videos, a workbook and everything you need to kick start your mindset. I wanted it to reach a the wide audience that had watched my life for the past 8 months as my husband's death played out in the UK press. I want those people to have hope too. I wanted them to have something basic, something that explained how on earth I was doing so well and being so happy, so soon after losing Ross.

The Happy Me Project was born and has been a huge success, I am now doing The Happy Me Project Live workshops around the country and meeting my large social media following in person. I have been appearing on Lorraine Kelly, a UK breakfast TV show and am being asked to get involved with projects all over the place. I have been asked to speak at some incredible events and I'm being featured in magazines and books over the next year.

Success to me is waking up every day and doing what I want, it's giving back and its living my life on my terms. I am already successful and realising that is empowering.

Now of course that doesn't mean I have no more plans or desires for future me, I plan to develop a self-development TV show, write my own book and build my brand even bigger over the course of the next year. I feel a pull back to the land of TV, but ultimately it must now be on my terms. I truly adore working with people and helping them to unlock their potential. I am fascinated by why we do things and why some people have amazing lives, whilst other constantly block their own way. I am obsessed with freedom and I want everyone to have it. I know more than ever now that life is horrifically short and I want to make a mark in that time, I want to give life a real good go. I don't feel sorry for myself, I have an incredible life and no matter how heartbreaking it has been to lose my best friend, the other half of Rolly, I know that he was happy with what he did. Ross always said to me that he had done everything he wanted to do and that he was happy. I don't think any of us can ask for more than that in life.

To those that are just starting out in their entrepreneurial journey my top tips are these; know what you want and the life you want but be flexible in your methods, stay loose as you never know what challenges may just make you have to change course. Don't be scared of this though, it's part of life and will make you stronger. Create boundaries, decide what your life rules are and be rigid on this, the boundaries stop you losing yourself along the way. You don't have to BE anyone but you, you are enough and if you try to be someone else, you will only ever be a poor version of them.

Don't play victim. Don't feel sorry for yourself, your life is no one's responsibility, but yours and people's opinions are none of your business.

I have had many setbacks in my working life, times when people probably thought I had lost my mind, but I always kept going, I always kept telling my truth and I knew what I wanted. I still know exactly what I want. I have also allowed myself the respect to change my mind when I want to. Just because I wanted something at 20, doesn't mean I want the same thing at 33.

I love my life and even through the tough stuff I have learnt, I have grown and it is all part of this journey. I don't take myself too seriously and even though I have no problem saying I am bloody good at what I do and people should definitely get around me, I know that life is all just one big game and can flip around in a second.

I cannot wait for what the next 12 months bring and look forward to working with some more incredible people.

# 8. SHERRY

Over the past 7 months I have undergone a complete transformation of mind and body. In this my story, I would like to share with you some of the challenges I have faced in my lifetime and what I feel it is that has enabled me to overcome these and find myself in the present moment which is one filled with peace, hopefulness, passion, gratitude and motivation. Earlier this year I was sat at the kitchen table and I realised I was soon to be 48. Then the bombshell struck, I was hurtling towards being 50 and in reality, I was in the worst shape I had ever been in since being a baby and fighting for my life.

Born 2 months early on 21 April 1969 weighing just 5lbs I came into the world in just the same way as my life was to unfold, on a mission. Although I initially gained strength and weight well and appeared to be thriving, I soon developed complications with my lungs and I began a battle to stay alive. At the age of 6 months I became a long-term patient at London's Great Ormond street hospital and my parents endured several occasions where they were told I would not make it. To my knowledge I was given end of life prayers by the duty Chaplain on no less than three occasions. At aged 18 months I underwent surgery to remove the majority of my right lung and although the main problem was removed I was still chronically asthmatic and prone to life threatening chest infections. It was my 'fighting spirit' that the consultants said kept me in the game. Every time there was an episode they would tell my parents I wouldn't make it to the next birthday and each time I reached it they gave them another date. After years of on off medical treatment I was finally allowed to go home and stay home ready for my third birthday and by the age of 10 after my last hospitalisation the doctors said anything after that was borrowed time. Well at aged 48 I am incredibly grateful that God has allowed me to stay and continues to have great plans for me.

I grew up in a loving family where my parents and siblings were a continued source of love and affection. I was a happy, sociable and conscientious child and apart from the usual teenage angst that we all go through I had a pretty normal adolescence. I married my childhood sweetheart at 19 whom I'd met at the age of 13 and we were married for 13 years and had two gorgeous boys. At the age or 32 the marriage broke down and I found myself adrift for the first time in my adult life after spending over half my life with this one person. Over the course of time, I had alienated myself from my family pretty much as the relationship between them and my husband wasn't great, through their eyes they had seen a happy, confident, self-assured girl lose herself to a self-critical, unavailable and often very sad replacement. The spark had gone and there was very little passion and zest for life left in my eyes. Don't get me wrong, I had achieved some great things in that time, giving birth and raising two beautiful boys for one. I remember as I child, my wish was to get married and raise a large family. I loved the idea of running a home that was filled with love and happiness and when I married in 1988 that is exactly how I thought it would pan out. In reality, it was not to be the case. Self-doubt and a lack of self-respect grew over the years and saw me accept things that in my younger years I would have never allowed to happen. An attempt to address this in-balance came in the form of me returning to university and becoming a teacher, securing a job I loved and living in my own house in my home town but I had in fact lost 'me'. It was at this point the I began to claim my life back, I rebuilt the closeness to my parents whom I saw all the time instead of occasionally as had been the general pattern over the preceding years. I reconnected with friends whose friendship I had neglected as I moved from place to place following my husband's career. Now I was living in my own home I was beginning to regain a sense of self and I remember how good it felt to know I was able to start thinking for myself again and make my own decisions. To embrace my new sense of independence, I decided to completely gut and redesign my bedroom to make it a place of beauty,

peace and restoration at the end of a hard day raising two boisterous boys under 3 and working part time as a teacher.

It was during this process I met a lady who has become one of my lifelong friends. I had ripped up the carpet and dismantled the rickety bedroom furniture, enjoying the exhilaration that resulted from the sheer physical effort needed but now had to find somewhere to dispose of it. Across the road was an empty skip in a neighbour's garden, a causal hello found me asking if I might add my things and the rest they as they say is history. Another chance meeting with her neighbour struck up the second friendship and with the addition of her neighbour we had ourselves a group of single girls who cemented friendships that would feed and support us for the next few years before we all moved. The 'Charlton Road Girls' as we called ourselves was definitely a lesson in how powerful positive relationships can be, surrounding yourself with people who support and up lift you makes you view the world very differently. Their friendships are a source of strength and positivity that remains to this day and although we see each other far less these days they will be friendships that remain with me forever. Life began to feel good again and I was certainly aware of the feeling that I was rediscovering who I was, thoughts and attitudes from when I was a girl would remind me of the kind of person I used to be and the things that made me happy and what I felt were important and made a difference. The need to want to help and take care of people became stronger and along with it came a desire to make a difference in people's' lives. My faith was again an important part of my life and I started to attend church regularly. I knew that part of living a good life was to help others and when 9/11 occurred the church were sending a volunteer party out to help with the soup kitchens. At this point I was faced with all the negativity again about what value to the world I had to offer. The boy's dad was unwillingly to look after them in order to allow me to go to America for 2 weeks and asked what I thought 'Sherry Paget' (as I was then) could do that would be of any help to the people at ground zero. I was crushed all over again, who did I think I was, why would I think I had anything to offer anybody, I hadn't been enough to keep a husband from wandering throughout my marriage and now I was on my own. Thankfully the love I received from family and friends gradually restored my belief in me and after changing jobs to a local school which was minutes away from our home I set about finishing the renovations of the house and making a loving home for the boys and I. Life felt good again, we were making memories and it was good, although the first time the boys spent the day and night away with their day was incredibly hard I soon found that respite every fortnight became time for me to relax and chill and rejuvenate. I spent time with the 'Charlton Road Girls' and I was truly on a journey of self-discovery. My parents visited often from their home in the West Country and on one such occasion I remember walking in on my mum crying, when I asked her what was wrong, she said she had heard me laughing in the other room and it was the first time in years she had heard that pure joyous belly laugh from me and she realised her 'daughter' was back. Over the next 10 years life saw me marry again and move my family to France, for many reasons this was a decision I would not take again if I had my time over but I made some life-long friendships and will be eternally grateful for those. Although the marriage was to fail, we are still very good friends and I have been able to see the ending of a relationship does not always have to result in conflict and aggression which leaves you stripped emotionally and with no self-confident. I was able to move on with a positive outlook and take the good emotions and thoughts with me. However, I did realise that I had the habit of allowing people to control my thoughts and actions and I never really strived to be in charge of my own destiny. I lost sight of what was important and in an attempt to please everyone I pleased no-one. I had allowed my faith to weaken and stopped living a life that centred around the teachings of Jesus. I believe that has an impact on the thoughts we have and the actions we carry out and as I tried again to please someone else and their expectations I lost sight of me for the second time. Emotionally I was at a low point and made decisions that at the time I thought were the correct ones and were best for those concerned rather than myself. The outcome was I set my life on a path that has since that day felt like second best. It was not in line with my childhood dreams and wishes and the sense of guilt has often been all consuming. Although outwardly nothing would appear awful to those around us, I know for me and my family the decision was wrong and even though the negative feelings are possibly only really felt by me, sometimes the pain is actually physical. I think, that comes from the realisation I cannot change the past and when I allow myself to face that head on it can literally feel like my heart is breaking. It is only recently as I have been on this journey of self-development that I can see it is something I need to deal with. I am beginning to face the fear of how it feels to deal with the feelings and finally learn to forgive myself and let the guilt go, without that process it is impossible to truly move on and fulfil the potential in life you were destined for. Despite not having a great sense of love for myself, life decided that love was to find me again and in October 2015 Scott proposed to me while we were on a trip to Las Vegas. I now share my life with someone who surrounds me with love and support and extends that to all those around me. He showed me what it was like to share your life with someone who wants the best for you and knows you better than you know yourself at times. There is no control, actions and words come from a place of mutual love and respect and a common goal to build a life together equally. When those around you love and support you, the best version of you emerges, and in the times when you are not at your best, their unconditional love carries you through any feels of doubt or guilt. That person doesn't have to be a partner, he can be a parent, sibling, dependent or friend, just someone you know that loves you unconditionally. I view my life so far as an incredible journey, and now as I write this at 48 I look back at how far I have come.

After a couple of really challenging years starting with being frighteningly close to losing my life again after 38 years I made the decision that things had to change. My life has had its share of ups and downs and challenges, starting from fighting for my life as a baby to falling into the depths of depression after losing my mum in Oct 2016. Losing her has to be the hardest thing in my life that I have been faced with for sure. Being 48 I really wasn't prepared for the feeling of being 'lost' that engulfed me. I may as well have been 10 years old. As I was growing up I always dreaded the thought of losing a parent but in recent years I began to accept it was part of life and although I knew it would be painful, I thought it would be a grieving process that I would go through just like anyone else and life would just carry. Wow, how wrong was I? I was totally unprepared, although I spent the last week of her life by her bedside awaiting the inevitable I actually never really accepted it was going to happen and when it did, I felt like I had died too. People kept saying it would get better and life would get back to 'normal' after the funeral. I was expected back to work the day after the funeral and I look back now and I think my mind was shutting down. On the day of the funeral I remember an overwhelming sense of complete numbness apart from just after I had done my reading. When I returned to the pew, the physical pain was unbearable, I felt like my chest was being crushed and for a few moments I truly thought I was dying and would be joining my mum. From that point on I sank deeper and deeper into a dark place, the doctor signed me off from work and I literally gave up. Life had no meaning, although I still had all the other people I loved around me I felt like a lost little girl. I cancelled my up-coming hen weekend and along with my dad we became pretty much like hermits not leaving the house. I spent the majority of the day crying and could speak to no-one as the words would not come out.

Our forth coming wedding was the only thing I could use to drag myself through each day. There had been thoughts of cancelling it but as a family we needed something positive to focus on and my mum would not have wanted me to change it. The day itself was beautiful and it gave everyone some much needed positivity. Mentally and emotionally I was not in the best place and the day actually felt very surreal for me, much like what I imagine an out of body experience would feel like. We went off on honeymoon and my dad went to stay with my brother for Christmas and New Year. Being away helped in many ways and the peace and tranquility of Bali fed my spirit in a way that is hard to describe. There is a sense of healing all round and as a non-Christian country Christmas is not celebrated which suited me just fine. Scott and I shared a quiet and intimate day and I was relieved not to have had to face the expectation of having fun and enjoyment for the first Christmas without Mum. The next morning, which was Christmas day in the UK, we received a call from my brother to say my dad had had a heart attack and was in hospital. Again, the world came crashing down, I was halfway around the world and in danger of losing my second parent in the space of months. We spend the next two days in limbo, after many reassures he was going to be fine we stayed for the remainder of our honeymoon and tried to make the best of it.

When we got home, I knew taking care of my dad was now my main priority. I believe it is my grit, determination and that 'fighting spirit' coupled with a genuine need to care and serve others that has enabled me to come through these life challenges. I have made some decisions I would not make again if I had my time again, but I believe your past is what brings you to the person you are in the present. I was a teacher for 20 years and very passionate about it, I finally left the teaching profession and my role as Head of a Pre-Prep department in February to become my dad's full-time carer. It was during the time between then and April I decided things had to change and I needed to look for a path that would reignite my dreams and passions which had been lost along the way. I have now embarked on a transformation from the inside out, refocusing on my mind and body. I have found a business that allows me to be at home with my dad and create a path to financial and time freedom, helping others around the world and I absolutely love it. 7 months into my journey I have lost 3 stone, look and feel better than I have in many years, come out of a very dark place and now live a life that brings me more happiness and inspiration than I thought possible. I am connecting with people globally and making a difference, ultimately, I will make a valuable contribution to the lives of many as my goal is to use my business to fund a charity that raises awareness of the increase in case of mental health issues in children. Whether my own or those who come in and out of my life, they always have been and always will be my passion.

# 9. LUCY

My start in life was a little less than smooth, my parents separated not long after I was born. I lived with my Grandparents throughout my early years, my mum worked full time and so it was mainly my Grandma and Grandad that cared for me. I have very few early memories of my mum. Looking back my parents separating was the best thing that could have happened, it gave me a chance in life, had they not separated I wouldn't be who I am or where I am today. I didn't meet my biological Dad until I was 21, he just recently passed away. Then one day my life as I knew it changed, my Mum had met someone and we moved to live in York. I can still feel that ache in my heart because I missed my Grandma and Grandad so much, they had been my constant. My sissy arrived not long after our move, I kid you not I've never felt so proud as the day I became a big sister, I mothered her from day one. Little did I know that one day I would actually be her mum! Things changed after Meg arrived, I remember so clearly how my parents argued and that I didn't like living in my house. I felt a huge sense of relief when they separated. Looking back that's an incredibly heavy thought for a 7-year-old to be having.

My mum seemed broken, I don't so much remember us laughing together or having fun. I just remember getting told off. A LOT! I think that this is probably when she started to really struggle with her mental health. Next came my step dad, that was an interesting time, I'm not afraid to admit that I hated him. I think I was 8 by this point and I felt so powerless in the situation, living with a man that loved both my mum and my sister, me not so much. It's a complicated relationship to explain, there were highs and lows, I grew to love him in the end but sometimes I beyond hated that Man. I found my teenage years tough, by this point my Mum had been struggling with mental ill health for quite some time, let me tell you that is NO easy thing to live with. I felt lonely, isolated and trapped. School was a getaway, I was full of character and had a great relationship with my teachers and had great friendships. The funny thing is they didn't really know me, I was incredibly embarrassed about who I was and where I had come from. During those school hours I got to be somebody different, I got to be happy and carefree. As an early teen I started to get this really weird feeling in the pit of my stomach, it made me feel physically sick, I now realise that's where my journey with anxiety began. It was at around this time I made myself a promise, a promise that I would never be ANYTHING like my parents. Still to this day I feel gratitude that they taught me the best way not to be a parent. My Grandparents kept me going, I spoke to them every day and I would visit them as much as I could. They always were my BIGGEST supporters. They loved me so much, I could never have been completely honest about how awful it was at home, it would have hurt them too much. I owe my life two these two amazing people. So I was in the thick of my GCSE'S and I realised that there was something really wrong with my Mum, beyond her depression and anxiety. I was starting to think that she had a drinking problem, I was on my own with that thought and it was very much brushed to one side. I kid you not she was a nightmare to live with, often 'asleep' on the sofa, she was always angry and the unkind things she said to me stuck with me for years.

Living this life was beginning to break me, I was so unhappy. I began to make myself sick, the first time it was an accident, but I liked it. I made myself sick multiple times a day for 3 years because it allowed me to be in control and I have no idea why but it gave me an escape. I hid it so well that nobody knew. Strangely once I started university, it just stopped, I didn't need to do it anymore, it was like a switch had flicked. I'm a pretty open person about most aspects of my early life but I struggle to talk about that. I moved to Sheffield, I'm actually still here 12 years later. It probably not surprising that I ended up in a relationship with a boy that treated me exactly the way that my Mum had, I stuck that out for way too long. The thing Is, I didn't feel worthy of unconditional love. Until one day David happened to walk into my life, and in that second my world completely changed.

I've blogged about this in the
past but seriously I knew from the moment that I met him that he would be the man that I married. I rarely went 'home', which was hard, I missed my sissy so much. I also struggled to maintain my friendships from school. By this point I was 21 and I was finding my feet within the adult world and I knew for CERTAIN that my Mum had a problem with alcohol, still nobody agreed with me. It's awful to say but I was beyond caring anymore. At this time my step Dad had an insane notion that everything would be better if they moved to New Zealand. It wasn't long after they decided to move that I got 'the' call. My mum had been admitted into hospital, her friend went on to explain that she had had an 'accident' at home and that her head had set on fire. For months saying the words 'my Mums head set on fire' actually made me laugh, people thought that I was crazy. Laughter was the only way I could respond to this outrageous thing that had happened, it didn't sound real to me. I sometimes wonder if I was in denial. When I got the call, I didn't rush to the hospital like you might think. I went home cried, ate a full box of chocolates and in that moment vowed to myself that nobody would be moving my sister to New Zealand.

My mum made a full recovery. My sissy however is still re-covering from the psychological trauma, she saved my Mum, I don't know that she'll ever come to terms with what happened that day. So I'd decided that I needed to keep Meg from moving to New Zealand whatever the cost, I knew it would be hard, but it was harder than I'd ever imagined. After only a few short months together David sat me down 'babe we'll do whatever it takes to look after your sister' In those words I knew that I'd met somebody pretty bloody special. The move was in full swing, I still remember calling my mum to tell her that Meg wasn't going and that she was coming to live with me. Strangely there wasn't the fight that I'd expected. I think she knew it was actually the right choice. My step Dad was livid, I didn't give a single shit. I wanted so much more for Meg, I didn't want her living through the struggles that I had and so at the age of 22 I became her carer. We got a flat, Meg studied for her A-levels, David went back to university as a mature student and I put my ambition of becoming a teacher to one side and worked full time as a waitress to keep us afloat.

It was during that time that I cut ties with my parents, my Mum was in a full-on spiral of self-destruction and my step Dad for a better word was a total dick. I couldn't fight anymore, crying had become part of my daily life, I was working my ass off and I felt so broken. It was one of the best decisions that I've ever made. For the first time in my life I felt FREE. Fast forward a few years and Meg was settled, so I decided to start studying to become a teacher. That Post Grad was relentless, I was doing a 4 hour round trip each day, I worked a 12 hour day on Saturdays and visited my Grandad on Sundays. David kept me going but my god I do not know how I got through that year. Graduating as a teacher in front of David, Grandad and Meg was such a proud moment, I struggled to keep it together as at this point we'd lost my Grandma. I loved that woman so much, she always rooted for me and I knew that she would have been so proud of me for achieving my dream career. That September brought new beginnings for us all, Meg moved to London to study at University, David became a specialist in helping physically disabled children and I started teaching at a school as an infant teacher. Things were coming together nicely, it felt a little bit like we'd served our time, lived through our fair share of shit and now we were on the up. We got married that summer, my Grandad gave me away, I became Mrs Tollerfield. That was huge for me.

Until I met David I had struggled a lot with my identity, I couldn't understand why my Biological Dad hadn't fought for me and so having his name felt empty. I was the only Warren in my family and I constantly felt like an outsider. The day I married David I knew that I would never not belong again. Not long after we were married my life fell apart, my Grandad died unexpectedly, the grief that I felt was incomprehensible. The man that chose my name, that taught me to ride a bike, that picked me up when I fell had gone. Gone. Never again would I sit on his knee, or kiss his sweet cheek, hold his hand or tell him that he was my favourite person in the whole world. I was really, very, totally, completely heartbroken.

The year that followed was a blur, we bought a house, I moved schools to be closer to home and we found out that we were pregnant with Rudi. Rudi Norman arrived and turned our life upside down, God I loved that kid with my every fibre but becoming a Mama was hard, much harder than I had ever imagined. I didn't have any family around to help me, my sissy was still studying in London and I felt really alone. I'm known to be a bit of a drama queen (my sissy calls me top DQ) but Rudi was the hardest baby, he really was. I was finding life really hard, constantly riddled with guilt, worry, inadequacy, I felt like I was letting Rudi and David down more each day. I couldn't think straight, making a decision was impossible and it sounds so silly now but I was convinced I was going to die. After months of hiding how I felt, I'm so good at that! I decided that I couldn't do it on my own, I admitted defeat and I went to see my GP. That woman saved me, she listened to me, she didn't judge me and she helped me get better at a pace that felt ok for me and helped me realise that it's OKAY NOT TO BE OKAY. I was suffering with Generalised and Health Anxiety, that's when it clicked that those feeling I had at school were also anxiety. I was embarrassed about what I was going through, I was really private about it and only told a few close people what I was going through. I couldn't even talk to my best friend, our relationship had become strained, much of that was down to me hiding what was going on and how bad things had become.

This is where I started to turn shit around, I made a crazy decision. I was going to leave my teaching profession, my once dream job suddenly seemed like a total nightmare. I wanted to raise Rudi myself, I wanted him to have early memories of me, to have me at sports day and on school trips. I couldn't bear the thought of missing out on those special memories. Leaving teaching felt like a weight had been lifted off my shoulders. So now I was almost 30, a Mama of a spirited boy and no career. While I didn't want to return to teaching I still wanted to generate an income and I still had a strong desire to be successful. I don't think I'll ever lose that feeling of needing to work hard to prove to other people that I am worthy. A series of events meant that I started my own Business in Network Marketing. Something that was totally 'not me' but it meant I could work from home around Rudi. It was an exciting time, little did I know that Network marketing would set me on a crazy journey of self-discovery and acceptance. I have learned to work hard on my mindset and personal development and have met some AMAZING people on my journey.

Not long after starting my business I found out that I was pregnant with Jesse Frank, throughout my pregnancy I was so nervous that he would be as hard as Rudi had been and that I'd go batshit crazy again. I continued to build my business and I felt so lucky that this time I wouldn't have the dread of returning to work. Once Jesse arrived we quickly discovered that he was a total dream, an actual textbook baby, 5 months in he's still a total gem. He was such an easy baby in those first few weeks that I carried on working on my business, I decided that I wanted to share my journey of building a business around motherhood and anxiety to help other Mama's know that they are not alone - the struggle is real. I really wanted to show Mama's that we do not have to conform to society's expectations and that as Mamas we DO NOT have to make a choice between motherhood and a successful career, I hate that we're led to believe they are our only two options. To that I raise 2 fingers. And so Mamarooandboy was created, I put my thoughts out to the world, which was scary as shit, but, I have had an amazing response to my blog topics. I found a social media mentor, he encouraged me to branch out on Facebook, join a few new groups to make new connections. 'Make connections, turn connections into friends, turn friends into family' was his advice to me. So I searched for a group that felt true to my journey, I came across Mums in Business Association. Never did I think that it would set my journey on a completely different road. I decided to put my Network Marketing business boots to one side to build my brand Mamarooandboy. I am currently collaborating with some amazing Mamas to launch a blog series called 'We are ALL Mama's'. The series focuses on real issues that Mamas face such as anxiety throughout pregnancy, becoming a mama to a child with additional needs, Raising twins, The struggles that come with Autism, the loss of a child, becoming a Mama without a Mama, being a single Mama, a working Mama. The list of topics is endless. Motherhood. It's hard, gritty at times whilst being totally amazing all at the same time, emotional rollercoaster much! Mamarooandboy is about raising awareness of society's view of Motherhood, the judgement and taboo topics. As a Mama collective we are all experiencing a different journey with the SAME job title, society holds us to an unfairly high standard, often with little support. It's time to make a CHANGE.

What does the future hold? Well, I am a firm believer that our journey is mapped out from day 1, it's up to us to break our boundaries and find our path to success. It's weird but I have always have a strong feeling that I was destined for success, it used to make my Grandad laugh, my total certainty of it. Norman until my very last breath I will work to make you and Grandma proud. I wanted to finish by explaining that I have absolutely NEVER been defined by my start in life, it has made me strong, I am a fighter and I will always strive to prove people wrong. I wouldn't be the person that I am today had I not lived through those experiences. I am also So lucky to have the never ending support of my best friend and husband David, my wingman! In recent years I have learned that personality, passion and a desire to succeed can move mountains, so while I'm not an academic genius, It doesn't matter.

I'm actually pretty certain that I passed my driving test because I pretended to have two dogs, and got onto my PGCE because I offered the interviewer a pretzel! I love to meet people, I've a lot of life banter to give and l Like I said, I have always had a crazy idea of becoming successful.

Please know that 'The only person stopping you is You'. Finally. I am a Mama, I make mistakes, I am human and that's Okay. How will your story end?

# 10. NAOMI

Before I jump right in telling you all about my journey, of changing my status from a young mom to a mom in business, let me introduce myself. I am Naomi Jade Francis the proud mother of two amazing princesses. I hold a degree in Marketing and Human Resources Management and recently finished my studies as a Wedding Planner. Like every other young mother out there I have dealt with the challenges of being a young mom, fighting the stereotypes and finding myself. I am now the owner of Vintage Venue Styling a wedding and events venue stylist, working throughout the UK. My business is my passion and my girls are my life. It wasn't easy reaching where I am today and like others I battled my own self-doubt and against the discouragement from others but one thing for sure I am happy for my journey so far. I have learnt so much and have so much more to learn not just as a young mom but as a mom in business.

So, my journey....it all began in 2009. I can remember the weekend clearly it was towards the end of fresher's week and I had come home to see my family after settling into university. It was my first week studying and living away from my family. I had planned university for years, I couldn't wait to start and move out of my home like any other ambitious teenager. My Saturday had passed with me being in bed ill, I woke Sunday morning with an absolute pain tearing in my lower abdomen. I sat in the bathroom screaming in agony, my youngest brother passed the room telling me I sounded like I was having a baby. It never crossed my mind that I could be but as the pain got more intense I had the urge to push and passed out. I was woken to screams of my name and those around me telling me, that I had given birth to a baby girl. In my eyes, my life had turned upside down; what about university, my studies, my dreams everything was gone. My younger sister screamed at me that I was losing too much blood and if I didn't lie down I was going to bleed to death. My head was in a whirl, I had passed out, I had a baby, I was a mother, I was supposed to be studying at university, was I really about to die.

The ride to the hospital I barely remember, partially because I was in and out of consciousness. The minutes turned to hours as I sat in the hospital bed, family and midwives ran around me asking questions. I sat there lost, all I could think was why me? How could I allow myself to become a typical teenage mother? My area was statistically known for young parents and I was now one of them. Coming from a Christian upbringing, I knew straight away that questions would be asked. I felt I had let everyone down and the thought of that was harder than knowing I would be raising a child. It didn't take long before the comments and messages of disappoint started coming through. "Look what you have done", "life will never be the same" just some of the various comments I had to deal with. The midwife collected me in the evening to go and visit my daughter who had been whisked through the mayhem to neo-natal. As I walked in and saw her lying there with tubes and monitors my heart sank, I now no longer cared about statics, being a young parent or failure, this was my baby and she needed me.

I spent five days in the hospital, I found I had a lot of time to think and maybe over think. I was supposed to be in lecture back at university but instead, I was propped up in bed nursing my baby. University was now a memory of what I was going to do. Instead I was faced with the constant reminder that I was a mother, that I was no longer a teenager although I was eighteen and that no matter what my child came first. In times like this it is very easy to find yourself in a place you never imagined. Many nights were sleepless not due to my daughter but due to my mind in overdrive. If it wasn't for my faith in God and that nothing was too big for him to help me through I truly believe I would not have started out on this journey. I do believe that everyone needs something to help them through tough times. For some it's their family, others a quote or song but for me it was my faith in God.

The first two months were hard, I cried to sleep many sleepless nights. Hours sat on the bed with my mother crying that my life was over. My emotions were a yo-yo, I didn't want to lose her but how could I carry on. I never found it easy been a mom straight away like most moms it was difficult, some days I felt deflated at eighteen I was no longer doing what my other peers were. Clubbing was something I hadn't even tried and most my evenings were spent at home putting my baby to bed. Going to my local town centre I found difficult, why was everyone looking at me? Anxiety played on me for months I felt that everyone was speaking about me all the time, I was barely enjoying motherhood as I should. My mother never let me go into depression she would sit there for hours encouraging me telling me to get myself up, that life had just begun. Her strong faith in God was a constant reminder that nothing was too big and I needed to find my own belief and carry on. Some may say it was tough love but whatever it was it worked, I started to realise days and nights got easier, baby and I were getting into our own little routine. I picked my phone up and called my driving instructor, I need to drive I told him, I have a baby and I am going back to university. I reapplied for university closer to home to continue my studies in Marketing and HR and started preparing to take on university not only as a educated ambitious young lady but as a mom with a bigger dream and a bigger purpose.

University days were challenging, after spending hours in a lecture, I then went home to pick up my daughter. Unlike many of my peers I found my evening consisted of a child on my lap as I typed through each essay or assignment. With my hands full at home, getting work done was always a little difficult. I never had time to stay over at the library to get extra work finished and used the time I did when baby was asleep to complete what I could. Due to this I always had less faith in the work I handed in; was it good enough, did I even belong in university. There were times where the work was difficult and I didn't quite understand. I felt I was the only one going through this, it never helped that I already doubted my being there. Anxiety was also creeping in, never knowing whether peers wanted to be a friend or just pity you. I found myself being very conscience of everyone around me, because of this I didn't build the friendships I could have. There were times I could have easily quit, but then whenever I felt that way, the don't give up in me would creep up telling me that giving up wasn't my option. In my last year of university, I took up a new challenge of volunteering as a primary school mentor. The mentoring was very eye opening, as I was the youngest mentor on the team. My role was to mentor primary school girls as well as their parents. The girls mentoring was easy going, working on showing the girls the various paths they could take in the future. We would undertake weekly task, broadening their horizons and realising anything was possible. It was the parents that not only tested me but helped me to look at things differently. All of the mothers were much older than I but many had never studied or worked. I found myself offering advice on going back to education, building a better future and starting new careers. Helping others gave me another boost, being able to share my story made me realise how far I had actually come.

I never knew where I wanted to go after university, there were many career routes I could take but there was also so many opinions. I could work full time and put my daughter into after school, but then that was apparently abounding my child. I could work part time but then there were the financial issues it may cause and staying at home, well that was just plain lazy. I tried to apply for graduate roles but although I found myself getting through to interviews and even offered job roles due to the demanding schedules, I was unable to continue. I took a few other roles after I had left university but my family life never worked around them well. I decided to start a online clothing boutique with my sister who was studying fashion at the time. I was absolutely buzzing about the idea, after finding various wholesalers, making my website and compiling a social media following I was veering to go. Unfortunately, it was harder to get off the ground then we had expected. Sales were very slow at first and the buzz was starting to fade. I had spent quite a lot of money to start up, had registered as self-employed so was unable to claim any help. I still refused to give up so tried other avenues to sell, eBay, stalls and fashion shows. However, the business was just not moving, the support and interest was not there so eventually I claimed defeat and packed the business in. I was now back at square one. I eventually took a part time role working in compliance and governance for an insurance company. The role helped me build up more confidence, due to being responsible for not only my own workload but checking the work of others. Working as a valued member of a highly skilled team made me realise what I was truly capable of. My role was temporary but what I learnt was permanent. Although I enjoyed working within a company I was still looking for more, I started looking for a new venture I could take and there it was Vintage Venue Styling.

I was searching through Gumtree, simply flicking through the various sales in my local area. I came across an ad stating wedding business for sale, I clicked and instantly was drawn in. The ad was selling everything; business, website and stock. I felt this was perfect, something I had a interest in and was just there ready to go. I set up a meeting with the owner and got to know more about their business for sale. After our meeting, I was completely in love with the idea and could see where my university studies and experience of my job roles could help build this business into something great. I sat down and started weighing up the pros and cons, I turned to family and friends to get advice. However, I started to doubt myself could I run a business with a child, how would I manage been self-employed as well as look after my daughter. I had to first find the startup funds, I didn't want to put myself into another financial problem like the last business idea. My mother and aunt were happy with the business and could see its potential they therefore offered me the startup funds and Vintage Venue Styling became my new business. We signed in the June 2016 and I couldn't be more ecstatic, I was ready to go. My mindset was changed, regardless of what had been said, or what I had thought I was prepared. Maybe it was due to the startup of the business already been set up taking away the fear factor either way I was ready. I woke the next day to my first enquiry through the website. I squealed with happiness and emailed the client straight away, they called me and ordered a post box for his daughter's wedding. It was one order but I already felt I had made it. It didn't take long before the orders started coming through. By the end of July, I had five weddings booked. As much as they were small I was absolutely loving my new role. Even though my finances weren't building up as quick as I wanted the extra income was making life a little more breathable. I had eventually undertaken my first wedding, I enjoyed every part of it, setting up the room and seeing the end result was highly satisfying.

Over the coming months, the business went from strength to strength. I found myself hiring my wedding items out not just in my local area within the West Midlands but all the way to Hampton Court Palace Golf Course in London. The more weddings I undertook the more places I got to visit, each venue more luxurious. I was enjoying travelling to new areas, it broadened my vision of where I could take my business. I started to build a social media following, meet others in the wedding industry and started to build a name for myself. As each day passed, I became more independent within my business, some days there were still a struggle juggling parenthood with the wedding demands. I had found myself at last, I knew what I wanted to do. Naomi Jade Francis was a wedding venue stylist and loving it. No matter the scale of weddings I had to do, the enquiries, social media posts to make, wedding stock to update I was always a mother first. I would take my daughter with me to the odd wedding, helping me set up the various venues. We were the perfect mother and daughter team.

Fast forward a year later and I became the mother to another beautiful girl. It was instantly seen as another challenge and to others another mistake. How could I have let myself go back to where I was in 2009. I wasn't very prepared and had many weddings booked throughout the summer. Straight away the doubt and fear wanted to creep up again. How was I going to run my business with two children now? Once again, the rumours and Chinese whispers spread like wildfire. I could feel myself slowly going back to where I was 8 years ago, somewhere I had worked so hard to move from and build me to the person I was today. The comments hurt more this time round, no one seemed to see how far I had come in life. I had to look at life a lot different, I had to realise that no matter what people wanted to throw I had a lot in me to overcome it all and get back onto my journey. I truly believed that God would not give me too much that I could not handle and that everyone has something in life that builds them to who they would become, this was mine. I noticed that some close to me were slowly dropping in numbers, the most important part of me remained and that was God. A silent prayer to him was my help through this, it felt has though everything was lifted on my shoulder and gave me days where life felt settled. Although I was a mother it doesn't mean I couldn't handle anything. I had come so far with my daughter and business and now I had two which in my eyes meant I had another little helper to join the team.

I now look back to 2009 the young teenage mother with doubt, no idea what motherhood would bring and no self-belief. How she had grown, she overcome people's opinions of her, the doubters, gained confidence and had made something of herself. She was now enjoying life with two beautiful princesses, expanding her new-found passion her business and moving closer and closer to the financial freedom she has been working towards.

Age is nothing but a number, being a mother can come to anyone at any age and that does not define the future you can build for yourself. A mom in business is a mother nonetheless and that does not stop you from being the best. I now look at myself not as a young mom but a mom in business, a mom with a passion, a mom with a belief, a mom with beautiful children, a mom who is blessed and mom with not just a dream but a mom on an incredible journey.

# 11. KATIE C

I started my entrepreneurial journey young- my first business was at aged 18. I think I had always known this was the route for me and I loved it. It was a small sandwich bar. I loved it. My day consisted of going and getting everything ready for the day, prepping loads of sandwiches and loading them into my car. I then drove around various business parks and industrial parks locally and sold baguettes to all the people working there. I'd pull up and they'd come out and grab their favourite baguette or sandwich. Something, that to this day sticks in my head! If I see a customer, I still can reel off their favourite sandwich- sad I know! I started a catering business that I run from my sandwich bar at weekends for kids parties etc. Looking back- they were awful. Those hideous silver foil platters are not a good look, but it was another avenue to my business, that I loved. In the 2nd year, I had the opportunity to take over another sandwich bar, that hadn't been doing well, so I took a temporary lease on for 3 months, to see how I got on. Stressful was an understatement. I was trying to run the two sandwich bars with a few staff members, but I was running around like a headless chicken, trying to do it all pretty much myself. So, I had the first shop and those deliveries, then I'd dash down to the 2nd shop and stock up and do a delivery round in the town centre. I'd then go back up to the first shop for the lunchtime rush, then back down to the 2nd for the lunch time rush, that started a little later, close that shop, cash up, then back up the other one to cash up. I kept up at this rate for the 3-months and managed to triple the turnover of the second shop but my accountant looked closely at the numbers and even with those numbers, the town centre rates were so high, it didn't look like it would be viable, so I decided to go back to just the on shop. I remember crying my eyes out. I really felt like I'd failed as I hadn't done enough to make the 2 shops both work.

But that was nothing compared to the pain that I felt a few months later! I had booked a week's holiday and had staff that I trusted and that had been with me, pretty much from the beginning holding down the fort whilst I was away. I came back from holiday and literally with my suitcase still in my car from the airport- something made me drive straight to the shop. I had a niggling feeling. I walked in and something felt off. I went home and went over the takings over and over and something just wasn't adding up. Deep down, I knew that the staff member that I'd trusted had been taking money from the till. I felt completely devastated that somebody could do that to me, someone that I'd employed for nearly 3 years. The next day, after confirming this was the case, I obviously had to let her go. That's not an easy position for such a young person in business and it was the start of me not enjoying the business as much. A few months later, after 3 years, I sold the business and went into employment but toyed with coming back to self-employment constantly. I knew that I would inevitably end up back on that entrepreneurial rollercoaster.

Years later, after a holiday to Portugal, my now husband and I started another business- a guest house. We figured it was the perfect idyllic lifestyle to bring up children, but still run a business. We couldn't have been more wrong! We got the keys to a property that wasn't a guest house at the time, walked in (I was at this stage 3 months pregnant) and thought what the hell have we just done!

My husband and dad worked tirelessly for 3-months solid to

get the house renovated into a guest house and built all the en-suites. We took a booking- our very first booking from a family that booked out our 3 guest rooms, so we had no choice but to be ready in time! I remember one evening, I must have been 5-6 months pregnant, we had my 3 step children with us- who were little at the time, my friend dropped over her few month-old baby who I was looking after for the night. The very last nail in some floorboards went straight through a water pipe and there was water everywhere! After that crisis and an emergency call out, we were all lying in bed early the next morning and part of the ceiling fell down- it was one thing after another. But somehow, through sheer grit and determination, we opened up on time for our first booking and had some amazing guests with us over the years. Some stayed with us Mon-Fri for over 2 years, so literally became part of the family. Even watching TV in the guest lounge with a baby on their lap at times!

We also ran a catering business alongside the guesthouse, that thankfully, due to my husband who is an amazing cook, was a million times nicer than my little catering attempt a few years previous. My pregnancy was fine up until 34 weeks, when I was rushed to hospital with eclampsia, apparently close to slipping into a coma with dangerously high blood pressure. 2 hours after arriving at hospital, our little boy was born at just under 4lb - 6 weeks early. I was on the high-dependency ward and our son in neo-natal. It was a tough time, when I was allowed home, without my son and after my emergency C-section, it was straight back to doing the guest rooms. Luckily my husband was at home running the business full time with me, so he took on most of the responsibilities and my mum done loads for us too, whilst my husband would run me back and forth the hospital every 2.5hrs to feed our son. Luckily, our son made a rapid improvement and we were both allowed home together when he was 10 days old- he was tiny! We had some fantastic times at the guest house and after a wedding and another baby, both within 21 months of our first son being born, life was a complete and utter whirlwind. We also ran a catering business alongside the guesthouse, that thankfully, due to my husband who is an amazing cook, was a million times better than my little catering attempt a few years previous. After 5 years, 2 difficult pregnancies and 100's of guests, the guest house life became too much, too draining and we decided to sell up. At this stage, we knew I would continue to run my own business, but didn't know what. After much research, I decided that I'd start a Shabby Chic & Vintage Home & Gift online business and my '3rd baby' was born. This was started from our kitchen worktop, where I did everything by myself and grew the business using social media. The stock was small at first and was stored in my children's wardrobe. Each day, I'd have 2 1/4 hours whilst the little ones were at pre-school to pack and post any orders that I'd received and work on growing the business. I had a phenomenal first Christmas thanks to a product that sold like hot-cakes and not many people were selling at the time and the business was really taking off. We moved to a bigger house- predominantly so I had more room to house the now growing stock and I had a large office and a stock room followed by staff. I moved twice more to a business unit, then another, double the size as the business continued to grow at a fast rate.

I started another side to the business- literally, overnight- a monthly box subscription that took off in month 1 and was going amazingly well. It was a box containing lots of little gifts, trinkets, stationary- gorgeous bits & pieces. I loved running both sides of the business.

In 2014, I graduated with a Merit at Cardiff University - Foundation Degree in Social Media. Social media was how I had grown my business this far, and I knew this was the way of the world, so wanted to learn as much as I possibly could about it. I didn't go to university after my A Levels - opting, as I said to go into employment- followed by my own business a few months later, so this was a big deal for me. I felt extremely proud that I had gained a foundation degree around running a business and 2 small children. Although I was gutted I didn't get a Distinction! In October 2015, my husband and I went on an amazing business trip to China to start importing products direct, rather than through UK wholesalers. Through the company we used, I had an office in China, where they represented me and dealt directly with the manufacturers on my behalf. It literally was a trip of a lifetime and I was taking this business to the next step! In November 2015, I won a 'Mumpreneur' boost business award. The event was full of the most inspiring business women and I didn't really think I had much chance of winning at all. It was quite surreal, as I had 3-4 people recognise me as the face of my business or the name of the business, that I had displayed on my badge. They had bought from me and came over to say hi- a really strange but lovely experience! My husband was recording the award that I was up for and I remember the butterflies as they read out the finalists that were up for the award. When 2nd place had gone, I thought that it was definitely game-over, so when I won and Caprice presented me with my award I couldn't have been happier! A definite high point!

So, it looked like the business was going great guns. But I wasn't. Something had changed in me. To this day, I don't know exactly what, but I felt like I'd 'lost my mojo'. This had been my baby for almost 5 years, that I'd literally 'ate, breathed and slept' and all of a sudden, I wasn't in love with it anymore. This was a difficult thing to accept as I have always had that fear of failure niggling at the back of my head. I kept quiet for a while but could feel the stress building. The business started getting a little bit quieter- and that also made me feel extremely stressed. Looking back, I can see that it was predominantly my mindset that was affecting the business, but at the time I couldn't see the wood for the trees. It was a downward spiral. I was completely overwhelmed, trying to do it all myself and not spending enough time ON my business, but too much IN the business. I wasn't growing. When I (finally) opened up to my husband - he was amazing. Fantastically supportive. I had so many fears that he wouldn't understand and would feel that I'd not involved him sooner in the way I was feeling. But he literally told me 'just walk if it's making you feel like this, it's not good for you and we'll deal with the consequences together'. I think it was knowing that I had his support that fired up something in me that hadn't shown up for a while (the fighting spirit) and I decided that, hold on, I had a bloody viable business that I could sell- not walk away from! This was turning over multi six-figures and had an amazing following and good profit- I wasn't walking anywhere! So, I listed the business on a business for sale site (still among feelings of failure, that nobody would be interested etc.) and had around 40 enquiries in total. Those first few days I had 2 people come down to view and both wanted to make an offer.

The first offer came the next day, I accepted and I pushed for a sale within a month! The other interested party told me they were about to make an offer too, but I'd happily accepted the first offer. It was one of the hardest months of my life but we did it. The business was all in my head, I didn't have processes and systems written down, so all that had to be done. My husband had been telling me this for as long as I remember, but I always felt that I didn't have time. It was enough just dealing with the day to day running of the business and I guess I never thought I'd end up selling it! The new owner done her due diligence and she spent as much time as she could be shadowing me at my premises so she could learn as much as possible from me. It's amazing how much information you store in your head without really realising it. After the month, I'd moved out of my premises and the new owner had hers. I worked closely with her for months making sure the handover went smoothly and spent the six weeks holidays just being 'mum'! I took the 6-weeks summer holidays off to spend with my children and work on starting another business in the background! The new owner is a lovely lady and we luckily got on really well.

The business is still running today. I must admit, it took a while to stop thinking of the business as mine, but I'll always be the founder! The night I sold, my husband took me out for a gorgeous meal and lots of pink champagne to celebrate (oh, and some beautiful diamond earrings!). I felt so many different emotions, but the overriding feeling, was of joy. I knew that this was the right thing for me. I was sad that the business wasn't mine, but was looking forward to the future! It took me the best part of a year to realise that actually, I hadn't failed. I had started and sold a business for a profit. Being in that position made me think that I couldn't be the only woman struggling with it all- the kids, the house, the business. I couldn't be the only women trying to be the best at it all, but not actually believing in herself enough and what skills she could offer. I decided I wanted to help other women who were feeling that overwhelm, the pressure, the doubt, the lack of skills. So, I started another business as a VA.

At first, I didn't know what a VA was or that the role even existed. I literally wanted to help other women with the tasks they couldn't do, didn't enjoy doing or didn't have time to do. I didn't realise that it already had a label!

The more entrepreneurs I spoke to, the more I realised that many business owners felt this same way. I created my own website, set up my social media channels and started working on creating my new business. As the year progressed I started thinking that maybe I could mentor women, but the doubt stopped me from doing too much about that. I love working as a VA and as I became more confident in the skills I could offer (and put my pricing up), I started to really attract my tribe. I changed my website to be a reflection of me- I'm girlie and wanted it to show that. I started being really strict with who I was working with. Female entrepreneurs only. As time went on, I started to naturally attract a few coaches. This is such a positive place to be - full of inspiration and motivation- I spend much of my days being surrounded by amazing, like-minded, kicking-ass women! This made me realise that I can do this, I have plenty of experience and skills that women could learn from. I know I'm now on the right path, I feel it deeply and am so looking forward to the coming months and years. Continuing to grow as a person and continuing to help many women reach that same satisfied place. When I invested in me and my growth, I could feel the shift. Working with coaches, reading self-development books, working on my mindset has had a really positive change in me.

I now realise all my experience can actually be used to help other women that are also feeling overwhelmed and don't know where to turn. I know success means different things to different people. Let's be clear, I am money driven and I want to be financially abundant. But it's more than that, it runs so much deeper. This past year I have run a viable business that I love, doing something that makes me happy, helping female entrepreneurs, all whilst taking my kids to school every day, picking them up every day, never missing a school concert or event. I've travelled 6 times these past 8 months and managed my work around that. I've certainly drank more wine than I should have and eaten amazing food (hence the additional stone I'm carrying). I help women daily with helping them get clear on what they need to do to move forward. I'm happy and loving life. And to me that is in part, success. That is what I'm set on continuing with my life. I want to continue building my business, helping amazing women with theirs, be there for my children and family and above all be happy. I want to engrain into the minds of my children and step children that happiness is the no.1 priority. Life is too short to be living a life that you don't enjoy and the opportunities that are available to us all now are phenomenal. I hope you enjoyed reading a bit more about me. I know I love reading other people's stories, so hopefully, mine can inspire one or two of you too.

# 12. ANA

I've always been entrepreneurial, growing up around my dad it would be hard not to! I've wanted to work for myself since I was at least 18, I started network marketing then but had no clue what it was, I just did not want to work in an office. I went to drama school shortly after which I loved! Being active all day, sometimes 9-9 long days but doing what I loved. During my second year of drama school while studying in Barcelona for a semester I found out that I was pregnant with Nathaniel. I finished the year through with a very big bump and planned to defer a year and return when he was one. During my first year of being a mum I started working in a pub, weekends and evenings being away from my tiny baby was not fun at all. When I had to ring in sick one day to look after him, I felt so guilty that I decided something had to change. Then I partnered with a cosmetic company, this meant doing parties, still being away from my baby. It wasn't long until I found out that I was pregnant again. My plans to return to drama school faded, but we got offered a house and my partner, at the time, got offered a PGCE (teaching degree) but it was 60 miles away. We agreed I'd take the house and he'd take the PGCE and come back on weekends. Just before we moved in to our new two bed house we found out that I was expecting not just one baby, but two babies! Twins! With my massive bump and being on my own with Nathaniel during the week there was no way I could continue to do home parties. Being on my own in the evenings left me completely bored out of my brain and I needed something to keep busy but I had so little money. I had an idea to get creative up cycling from old

CDs, jam jars, glass bottles and used to go to car boots looking for second hand tea cups and saucers. I absolutely loved it and called it 'Rein vintage' I had so much fun doing it and going to stall events to sell them but I just didn't make money from it and once the twins arrived I went from having all evening to myself to being totally consumed in newborn babies.

It wasn't till the twins were 3 months old and Nathaniel was 18 months that I would a network marketing company that worked for me. I could do it all online from home around my three babies, I didn't need to leave my sofa it was amazing! Now I started to make friendships and help people it made me happy and kept me busy, so when my 'then partner' came home on the weekends because I wasn't sat on the sofa watching TV and I was on my phone busy working my business it made the problems in our relationship even more clear. It wasn't long after that I decided I didn't want him to come back anymore, it was a toxic relationship that wasn't good to be around the children and I knew we could cope just me and my boys. I was having an amazing time, I was growing as a mother and finding who I was again, my confidence was soaring as I was hitting promotions and my team was growing and my clients were getting amazing results. But like every journey it had ups and downs. After almost two years of being stuck at the same position in my company, not managing to get out of the ditch, life got that bit more difficult. My twins were showing that they were underdeveloped in their two year checkup, especially in their speech and language. It was a long 13 months of tests and no help, coping on our own, trying to deal with two very frustrated little boys who had no way of communicating with us.

I'm not afraid to say this but I completely took my eye off of my business, I was consumed with so many feelings and I was living in what I called "limbo" not knowing what was going on. I started doing some soul searching, I felt lost, my fire had burned out and I didn't really know what I wanted anymore. I was completely drained. I spent time doing a lot of law of attraction work, doing business and social media courses, trying to find my own way by building my brand 'BootyCamp Ltd' and just giving value to other people, I started to want to wake up early to work my business again. I built on this, I devoted my time to this, motivating other ladies helped to motivate me and I got my qualification in fitness instructing. It wasn't until May 2017 that we finally got a diagnosis for the twins they are both on the autistic spectrum and hearing those words was a massive shock (like literally no one had mentioned this to us!) but a huge weight lifted from my shoulders. Since then we have had so much more help for the boys, Jude's speech has come on from saying a few words to copying most words and being able to count to 50 and do the whole of the alphabet! Luca still has no words but he is communicating in his own way and he is interacting so much more with other people and has understanding of emotions. After being single for 3 years I've manifested myself the most amazing man, who completely loves my boys as he does me and we are now engaged and expecting baby no. 4! As for business, I partnered with a beautiful company which is filling my heart with so much joy to be able to help ladies feel fabulous from the outside as well as the inside and BootyCamp is going strong, we're working on igniting the fire within and helping ladies find their confidence. I will also be a part of the amazing MIBA's retreat in May 2018 so I hope to see a lot of you there.

From one mother to another, they'll always be bad days, days where you stink of poop or there's toothpaste all over the walls or you've been up all night with one kid and up early hours with another but they're all part of the package, never give up, just take a breather and remember why you're doing this in the first place. With love & gratitude, Ana Louise Bonasera

# 13. LAURA

I grew up on a council estates to parents that had worked hard their entire lives just to make ends meet. I started my first job at 14 which gave me my first taste of financial freedom and by 19 I had found the job I absolutely loved which was working in a nursery with children. I worked in my first nursery for 4 years but as much as I loved the job I was never quite satisfied with how overworked we were and by the time I was 20 and moved into my own home minimum wage just didn't pay the bills. That's when I was first approached by a rep for a network marketing company. Now I have to point out at this stage I was working full time and barely scraping by for the bills let alone able to put food on my table, I was desperate!

Over the next year I attempted to build the mlm business but it seemed to burn up what little money I had left in holding stock and buying everything I was told "was needed" to be successful. I made about every mistake that a newbie network marketer can make. Looking back I wince BUT I learnt a lot about myself in that year and it was the driving force that made me see that speck of potential even if I didn't have the know how. In the following 4 years I changed companies a total of 4 times and each company still has a special place for me. I met some great networkers, developed myself in ways I never knew I could and learnt some important networking tips, habit and traits. I still struggled to make them really successful but my saving grace I believe is my thirst for knowledge, if I don't know a thing I will learn it. Despite my personal development something was still missing. I couldn't put my finger on it.

Becoming a mother changed it all.....

I gave birth to my daughter in september of 2016 and quickly found babies were very expensive to keep. I had a little spark of inspiration when I went into a brand shop and saw an item on sale for 79p down from £18!! Now I was under no illusion that this store would not sell at a loss and if that was the type of markup they had then surely I could offer better!

During the sleepless nights of newborn hood I spent hours scrolling through wholesalers and website designs, laptop on one arm and baby feeding in the other, until finally I had a basic website with some nice products that were good quality without the brand prices. It was hard work, with a newborn baby and family felt as if I pushed them to the side but I had a vision and became so tunnel visioned that even my partner became 3rd in line after the baby and business. Looking back I think there's a strong possibility that I hid myself from the fact that I could have postnatal depression. After a big fallout with my fiance and facing life as a single parent i finally took the steps to help my own mindset and restart my healthy thoughts and actions. Gratitude journals, yoga and meditation alongside a great mindset coach and daily schedule meant my work life and homelife was becoming balanced, happy and healthy again. Over the next few months the business was gaining followers at an amazing rate and then sales and I was receiving great feedback on the products. I planned the start up to have limited overheads and before I knew it the company was earning pure profit. It was then that I started planning how to push things forward and it dawned on me that I had 5 years of experience in 4 different network marketing companies under my belt, 5 years of trainings and learning and self development, why not put that to better use?

So with my newfound epiphany I decided to put my networking skills and knowledge of how the companies run to re-launch as an MLM company and open it's doors to distributors. My goal was to create a company that always put it's reps and customers above profit margin. Not only did I want to help by providing a source of income and support I also wanted to support other working mums, dads and families trying to make a living and spend more time at home. This is how our Handmade by Mums range came to be. This range is our best selling and we now have great suppliers of absolutely amazing products, all made at home, and a great relationship which each of them. Not only are we benefitting our reps and families we work with but being parents we aim to provide families with what they really need.

The reception has been absolutely amazing! I soon had a team of absolutely amazing reps that worked hard and despite some never having been in networking before they were soon leading teams and duplicating my knowledge down. I receive daily compliments on how amazing the products are and I can officially say that the council estate girl that was making ends meet is an Official founder and CEO of her own company and inspiring people on a daily basis.

I now love spending my time growing our company, giving our reps an opportunity to earn, learn and grow and more importantly i get to spend my days with my daughter instead of heading out to the daily grind each morning. I can honestly say that i wake up in disbelief but proud and so motivated every morning, not just to succeed in business but to succeed in making and maintaining the company my reps deserve.

My biggest inspiration, product tester and company developer is my 1 year old daughter! As she grows and we discovered more about parenting so does the business grow and it continues to grow with her as i learn what being a parent is all about. I am getting there and all it took was a huge leap of faith and digging deep to find the self belief I never realised was there. I still have a lot to learn and it's certainly not going to be an easy ride from here but if I can say that I've helped 1, 5, 500, 5,000 people to make their dreams a reality, to gain financial freedom or simply say that I helped them find that self belief then it's all been worth it. There will always be trials along the way but with the right support system (or pure stubbornness) you can do anything you put your mind to.

# 14. MAGGIE

"Life is imperfect. It's beautiful and complicated and burdensome and messy and you are a part of it. A part that grows and changes and laughs and loves and gets broken and comes back together. But there will never be a time when you can't just step back and start all over."

Something which I, myself, am the epitome of.

My name is Maggie Cavanagh. I'm a Mum of 3 (Courtney- 19, Chloe-17 and Nathan-11). I'm a young Glam-ma to a 2-year-old mini-diva – Ariella and I am a Badass Mum in Business.

I've lived two lives inside of one, I am thankful for both.

I was a child from a broken marriage, whose Mum as the sole carer, did the best she could for my siblings and I (and still does to this day.) We have always been cared for, supported and loved beyond measure. At the age of 12, I was introduced to the man who is very much my Dad today. I grew up in a household where domestic violence was the norm and it occurred in our house on a regular basis, with me often having to protect my siblings from events we should never have witnessed. It was also back when it wasn't frowned upon to smack your children and as a tyke and a bit of a rebel I experienced that smack on a regular basis. In fact, many a time, I'd even accept it when it wasn't mine to get, to protect my younger siblings. It's only nowadays we realise how wrong this was and is. Family life is very different now to how it was back then. Thankfully, as I would not raise my children in that environment.

Anyway, as an astute, articulate academic I set about education in high school thinking I already knew all there was to learn and being disruptive. But no lesson could have prepared me for the heartache I'd experience with my childhood sweetheart, we will call him S, my first love. S was the school clown, the bad boy and although a little, shall we say hot tempered – he was loving and protective and in time I would learn a great Dad. At first our relationship was good, then it was great and then as adult life begun so did the arguing and the 'domestic violence history' I'd experienced as a child was to be 'hereditary' - but not for all of my life. S, was often in and out of prison for silly criminal charges and each time something else happened he would make the same promise of "I'm going to change". However, in hindsight, the time he had to make that change was limited.

I was never meant to be the type of woman who was an ongoing domestic abuse victim. But little did I know that in 2000, life as I knew it would change forever and it would have an impact on me that I would carry forward throughout the rest of my life.

On 8t h May 2000 my childhood sweetheart, S, attacked me in front of my parents' house, in broad daylight, in view of my family, their neighbours and my 2-year-old daughter, Courtney. To my defense, the two boys who lived next door to my parents' house and my Dad began to scuffle with S and a few short, life altering minutes later, S lay in my arms in the middle of the road, gargling and taking his last breaths. Life as I knew it would never be the same. Someone was watching over me that day. I whole -heartedly believe it would have been me if he had gotten his way. In the days later, I discovered I was pregnant with another baby, another daughter. A part of him that I'd keep with me forever. In January 2001 Chloe was born. I've always believed that she was a gift to get me through the months that followed.

The next few years were a blur of high court cases, losing my Dad to prison life, seeing my family being separated and torn apart, being a single mum of 2 daughters at age 20. I ended up homeless, my recreational lifestyle was drink, drugs and promiscuity and it took priority over everything else. I had completely lost myself and any advice or guidance went in one ear and out the other. I had jumped into a downward spiral. Was this the path that was laid out for me? Was this all my life would come to? I found that hard to accept but I did little to nothing to make any changes. The statistics of a person having experienced my life until then pointed towards the route that I was on.

But, being strong willed – or stubborn! I flung myself into proving the naysayers and gossipers wrong; "Ah, she won't amount to anything",
"She's just another teen mum, 2 kids at her age",
"There's that girl whose fiancé was murdered, she will never cope"

I thought in 2003 when I decided I'd had enough and would change my life around, that it would be the pivotal point in my life. I experienced an Ah ha moment that I believe almost everyone experiences. I'd found what I thought was my life purpose and I went about giving it away... isn't that the meaning of life?

I went to College and University. I Volunteered. I went from relationship to relationship, never letting down my barriers or getting too close to anyone for fear of being hurt. In 2006, I had another child, my son – Nathan. I did everything my big heart thought I should... This was it, I'd changed my life.... whilst I may have changed it from the turmoil I had experienced in my past, it wasn't for the better!

I masked my pain by working 100+hour weeks and ignoring many warnings that I'd burn myself out and have a nervous breakdown... it's just a figure of speech, right? It wouldn't happen to me. Not strong minded, big hearted, 'as long as I am helping others I'll be ok' Maggie! The thing is, it did!

Change is the only Constant. I once heard this quote and it really resonated with me. It's something I've kept with me since. As someone who has Adjustment Disorder this concept was one which although I kept with me, was a struggle to accept.

After believing for so many years that I'd had my fair share of the trauma life could throw at me, in July 2014 my whole life as I knew it, again overnight was changed and continued to fall away from me up to the point I lost myself... literally, I did not know my own name! I was broken and admitted to psychiatric care.

Having carried so many burdens for so many years, the last load was too heavy for my mind to carry. The love of my life, the man whom I thought I could let all of my walls down with, who I experienced true love with and who had finally shown me what real men should be like – turned out to be the catalyst of my world crashing down on me. Whilst on a family holiday in Bulgaria in June 2014, I discovered that he was not a one-woman man. As we stepped off the plane in Glasgow I felt like I had entered a parallel universe. I knew something had happened mentally and I felt like our relationship and my life with him had been one big lie. What ensued was weeks of absolute heartbreak, zig zagging between wanting answers and being able to forgive him and hating him and never wanting to see him again. It was all a mind game and eventually, it was one that beat me.

Physically, Mentally, Spiritually and Financially, I was destitute. I had given up my will to live. I had no desire to live in a world as the person I had become. Alone and scared doesn't come close to how I felt. I was unreachable and I felt like I had already died. The body still here was a shell. I told my mum on a daily basis that she was selfish for wanting me to stay alive. If she loved me she would let me die. I often hear people say that 'suicide is selfish': When you are over that edge; in your mind, there are no other options. Only people who have been there will ever understand.

Now, many people would think "Oh my! How could you cope?", "That must have been awful!" And I wouldn't disagree, however;

ON REFLECTION - I WOULDN'T CHANGE A SINGLE THING.
Whilst it took me a few months to begin to adjust, that breakdown saved my life. I feel like I was re-born. It's why I say I have lived two lives inside of one and I AM thankful for both.

Prior to 2014, I was diagnosed as having Bipolar Disorder. I was also the girl who 'had it all' I had the high flying successful career, loving relationship, 3 beautiful children, my own house, a huge friendship circle and I was an outgoing social butterfly.

I was also stressed, miserable, taking a plethora of anxiety medication, self-medicating, diagnosed with a heart condition; aggravated by my lifestyle, unfit, unhealthy and told I could anticipate an early death if I continued this way of life. Most shockingly being suicidal, that newsflash was music to my ears.

At 33 years old, I was so fed up, exhausted, mentally unstable, unhealthy and detached from living a normal life that I was prepared to end it all! And tried on several occasions.

What a walking, talking, thoughtless mess I became. I was a ticking time bomb. Cue, June 2014 and my minds own ability to shut down! What a great protection mechanism! Right?

During the last 6 months of 2014, I was placed into in-patient psychiatric care then community crisis care. During this time, the Bipolar diagnosis (or label) was re-assessed as PTSD, OCD, Agoraphobia, Adjustment Disorder, Depression and Border-line Personality Disorder. Quite a few new labels, although at the time I didn't comprehend any of this.

My mind decided to take itself on a well-earned holiday. When it returned, it was evidently well rested, had, had an epiphany and had been inspired to live, love and matter. The Maggie I was prior to June 2014 was gone. (And good riddance)

On reflection, I wasn't who I was supposed to be. I was diagnosed (wrongly) as Bipolar until that fateful day I broke. Back then I was unhappy, a high achiever, a perfectionist, a control freak, a busy corporate career mum in insolvency, putting everything before my family and myself. I was existing not living. I was the woman whose childhood sweetheart was murdered and the woman whose daughter was a survivor of sexual assault and the woman whose love of her life traded her in for a younger model. I was still a victim of my circumstances. I wasn't me! I had become all of the things that in 2003, I promised myself I wouldn't. Only, I had hidden it all from the world. As an onlooker, anyone would have thought my life was perfect.

I came from a place of anger.

A great quote I love "How does one become a butterfly? You must want to fly so much that you are willing to give up being a caterpillar" - Trina Paulus

I wanted to fly!!!

I looked within. The answers to everything were inside of me. I had to go seek that little girl I had left behind, locked in a room of darkness, filled with hurt, guilt, grief and anger. Each day I had to take her by the hand and reassure her that everything would be ok if she would just step forward into the light.

Through many hours of counselling, therapy, personal development and tears, my life now is non-comparable to how it was in 2014. My road back to my light has been painful, scary, exciting, and fulfilling. I would not change any of it. I am a stronger woman because of it and for that I am eternally grateful.

December 2014 brought us the news that my daughter was having a baby girl all of her own and in June 2015 Ariella was born making me a 34-year-old Glam-ma. Her name means Lioness of God, Protector and Healer. I'd say she did just that. In just one life, I found another reason for being, My Why, Faith and Jesus.

Today I find myself successful in a new industry, prioritising myself and my family above all. I am a coach. I am an activist for women experiencing domestic violence, trauma or mental health. I help other women to become the person they are to become through transformation of the mind, body and soul and my own story is one I have the platform to share empathetically and compassionately from.

I come from a place of love.

I've lived two lives inside of one, I am thankful for both.

I am not who I am or where I am because it was easy, I am who I am and where I am because it was hard. I refuse to dim my light to become as dark as my past circumstances.

My wealth of experience in the corporate, public and voluntary sectors places me at the savvy end of the business acumen spectrum. All was not lost throughout my workaholic years. Transferable to building a successful business within the Network Marketing profession – Network Marketing was my saving grace whilst I rebuilt a new life. It showed me that I was of still value, that I was still able to contribute to life and society, that I was capable of so much more than I had previously given and that I could design a life I loved for myself and my family. Through this profession I gained skills and attributes that enabled me to mentor other entrepreneurs and businesses and - I am now in the infancy of launching my own Body Positive Lingerie and Sex Toy Company, La Divinita - whilst studying towards a PHD in Human Behaviour and Sexuality.

I attribute my journey of success so far, to seeing the dark side of life in my role in the insolvency sector and my volunteer experience with Citizen's Advice, Women's Aid and Rape Crisis, as well as having personal experience of domestic violence, trauma and mental health conditions. I can also attribute a lot of my success to a non-negotiable vision which is much more than personal reward.

My purpose is to enable women to feel and love their whole self, to inspire them to live their own truth and to empower them to know they are invaluable in their own life and purpose. I encourage all women to embrace their inner goddess and sexuality.

When not spending my free time with my family, I can usually be found trying to break a sweat in the gym or rejuvenating myself at a luxury spa. You will often find me volunteering at a charity or taking part in charitable sporting events such as Tough Mudder. You could say I like to shed the girly image to get down and dirty all in a worthy cause.

My ethos is still Live! Love! Matter! This is something I convey daily in all capacities in my life.

For me It's time to go from startup to thriving entrepreneur, in my business and coaching practice - it's time to buck the old paradigm of having to compromise, hustle, drive and strive to create success. I am craving and deserving of more ease and flow. It's time to listen to my feminine intuition more, to grow my business and to create a life I am totally in love with.

I understand now, how my beliefs were blocking me from the life I desired and how I can use my feminine intuition and mindset to consciously create my reality and take inspired action to design a life that truly sets my soul on fire. I am embracing the thrilling risk of authenticity. I am bold, I am fierce and I have found my true meaning and purpose.

Psychologically programming your mind for success requires not only a deep-set belief and vision but it also requires a reason WHY. Adversity gave me my WHY.

I set about to consciously create my life, on purpose. I decided to be the girl who wakes up every day with purpose and intent, who shows up and never gives up. Who believes that anything is possible and I am willing to work for it.

Leading from the front, my own life transformation from

where I found myself in 2014 to who I am today speaks volumes about my strength, character and determination to make a difference and to inspire others by example. I did not come this far, to only come this far. The events in my life, which have each brought with them lessons were for a reason. I believe that reason was to show me my life purpose.

So why tell you all of that? When it's so personal to me! To let you know that you never know when your life can change in an instant.

To impress upon you to stop waiting on the weekend, stop waiting Mondays, stop waiting until next month, stop waiting until never!!! Stop making excuses why you can't and start thinking of all the reasons you can.

Don't wait until your mind, body or soul goes on holiday, like mine did. Luckily, I had the determination and strength to cling onto 'the edge' of the despair cliff long enough to come back from it. Not everyone has that outcome.

Take that leap of faith. Your current circumstances are temporary, whether good or bad.

No matter what your past looks like or how scary the future may seem, if you chose to be bold, to be brave and to believe in yourself... You really start to focus on the magic of what life is and you will then realise that most of your worries and fears are bullshit.

As Gabby Bernstein says, "you move from living in the darkness while experiencing fleeting moments of light, to living in the light and experiencing fleeting moments of darkness."

I aspire to be an empowered woman with a vision and grace.

Soft-hearted but strong, self-aware and sure. Respected for my mind, admired for my heart and above all, always honest, open and raw.

Yes, I've been broken, Yes, I've been knocked down, but every day I look fear in the face and now I never run. Life has taught me that I can always get back up. I am unbreakable. I am a warrior and I will continue creating and living my life by design.

I am not a victim of my circumstances, I am who I chose to become.

This story is just a snippet of many chapters in my life; with many more of my story still to be written. There are so many blank pages to fill. The best part is, at any time – no matter what arises, I now know there will never be a time when I can't just step back and start all over.
And... So can you!

# 15. VAL

I've always valued the importance of enjoying work. I've never seen the point in doing something without being passionate about it. Don't think that I don't have bad days, I really do, but overall the good days outweigh the bad, and I'm sure this is because I enjoy my work. I understand that everyone needs an income, but I want to earn money by doing something that I love. It's a very simple idea, but it's one that has served me well.

So who is this woman who apparently enjoys what she does? I'm Val, aka Elizabeth and Imogen's mum. I'm also a London tour guide (so I'm paid to talk). I'm a company director for Brit Movie Tours and Traditional Tours UK and the author of the children's picture book Jasper the Fire Fighting Dragon. For the purpose of this book, I'm predominantly going to focus on my children's book.

You may already have spotted the common factor between being a mum, tour guide and an author: it is stories. I love stories and always have. Each of the three main areas of my life (being a mum, tour guide and an author) really requires the ability to tell a good story. Telling a story is basically gossiping about historical or fictional characters. I can do that!

Naturally I enjoy telling my children stories and, like lots of parents, in addition to reading to them, I often make up stories too. The stories normally involve something that has happened to us that day, or about my daughter's new favourite thing, and just occasionally the stories turn out to be something special.

A while ago, Elizabeth, who was then 2, asked me for a story about a dragon and a fire engine. I obliged and came up
with a story about a water breathing dragon called Jasper who
joined the Fire Brigade. Over the next few nights Elizabeth
kept on asking for the story, so it was retold and refined until
we came up with Jasper the Fire Fighting Dragon. Then, being
the precocious child that she still is, Elizabeth asked to see the
pictures. This presented a problem, as I can't draw. I tried making a book out of stapled together sheets of A4 printer paper,
but I couldn't get the images in my head onto the paper. It
just didn't work. But Elizabeth was insistent, and to be honest
once the idea had been planted, I was quite excited about the
prospect of presenting her with a colourful book.

So I started researching children's stories: I read articles, I went
on forums, I devoured author's websites and I searched for
any publisher or literary agent who would accept unsolicited
manuscripts. The general advice was 'if you want to give a
copy of the book to your children, then self-publish it while
they are still young enough to enjoy it.' I couldn't believe how
laborious it was to publish a book through the conventional
methods. Broadly speaking it can take three years for a literary
agent to take on a new writer; then another three years for a
publisher to purchase the book; then a further three years for
the publisher to work on the story and publish it. Nine years!?!
Elizabeth would be 11 years old by then, and of course that's
assuming that someone likes the story enough to actually give
it a go! We've all heard how many publishers initially rejected
Harry Potter and Paddington Bear. No, I couldn't take the risk.
I wanted to give a copy of the book to my daughter, so I was
going to do it myself!

Before committing myself, I decided to put the story away for a few months, to see if I was still excited by it after I'd had a break from it. At Christmas, I dug it out again and read it to Elizabeth. Guess what she asked me? 'Can I see the pictures Mummy?' So I decided to go for it. I contacted an award-winning illustrator, called Sarah-Leigh Wills, who clearly knew what she was doing (let's face it, one of us had to) and joined her waiting list of eager wannabe authors. She was able to illustrate my story in May, which conveniently coincided with my next baby's due date. So I decided to make the book my maternity project – in addition to having another baby!

The months passed, Imogen was born and my illustrator started working on my book. Finally, it was ready and I had a glossy copy of Jasper the Fire Fighting Dragon in my hands. I cannot describe the pride and joy that I felt when I presented a copy to Elizabeth. But I found that I wanted to share the story with other children as well. I started thinking about the research that I'd done all those months before, when I'd considered submitting the book to publishing companies.

I had previously been advised, by my illustrator, proof readers and printing companies, that the story was good enough to publish. But these were all people vying for my business – could I really trust them? After deciding that I had nothing to lose, I contacted a company that specialises in Print on Demand books. I uploaded the book onto their website and they put the book for sale on Amazon. They would take care of all the logistics of selling it for me. Perfect. I wouldn't have to fork out for a thousand copies of the book and store them in my attic. I wouldn't have to keep an endless supply of bubble wrap and envelops at home or run down to the post office whenever someone ordered a copy. All I had to do was wait for it to be discovered. Easier said than done!

My next challenge was getting the book out there. Let me pause for a moment to tell you something about Brit Movie Tours, one of the tour companies for which I'm a company director. There are two directors in the company, and it's successful because we each have different skill sets. My business partner, Lewis is amazing at marketing, and I'm good at researching and writing tour scripts. To sum up our respective roles he is responsible for getting us customers, while I am responsible for fulfilling the orders that he has generated. I'd never had anything to do with marketing before. But suddenly I found that my book had turned into another business which I was running on my own, while looking after a new born baby and a head-strong three-year-old. Never mind, if I wanted children to know about Jasper, then I simply had to learn.

So, where are books sold? In bookshops! As a general rule, bookshops won't touch self-published books - something that I didn't know when I started this process. Not to worry, Jasper the Fire Fighting Dragon is a children's book, if bookshops won't stock it, maybe children's shops and gift shops might be interested. I decided that the books unique selling point is that it's not in every single Waterstones around the country – making it great for purchasing as a gift: the chances are that they won't already have a copy!

So my girls and I started visiting independent children's shops to show them the book. I'm proud to say that Elizabeth is a very confident sales person. She bounds into the shop, holding the book, and thrusts it into the hands of whomever is behind the counter saying 'we've got a book about Jasper! Do you want to buy it?' Part of me wonders how much of my success in shops has been down to her, and the fact that the owners can't bring themselves to tell her no! But traipsing around shops with two small children in tow is very time consuming. I was aware that I wasn't going to be able to keep it up once my maternity leave finished. Additionally I was spending more money on petrol and parking than I made in book sales.

I needed to think bigger. So I sent copies of the book to tourist attractions, to book distribution companies, I even tracked down the woman who purchases books for the National Trust and sent a copy to her. I couldn't get a response out of any of them. But why would they respond? They're all very busy and they haven't heard of me or my book.

Feeling disheartened, I turned to mum's in various Facebook groups. I only had 6 weeks of maternity leave left. I knew that I had to get Jasper the Fire Fighting Dragon out there before going back to work, if I didn't then it would just disappear. I really didn't want that to happen. I poured out my heart to these Facebook groups. I asked them how I could get children to see my book. I am so proud to say that these mums, who I'd never met before, really came through for me. They were full of ideas, and seemed to really want me and my book to succeed: I was invited into schools, nurseries and play groups to read the book to the children. I was invited onto local radio to talk about the story. Bloggers offered to review the book for me. Basically stuff started to happen, and I discovered the power of social media. I know, I was ridiculously late joining the social media band wagon – but better late than never!

As more people heard about the book it became apparent that I had underestimated the story. As previously mentioned, Elizabeth and I came up with it because she had wanted a bedtime story about a dragon and a fire engine. But it turned out that we had created a didactic story that really resonated with several minority groups, but was also popular with children in general. The story follows a water breathing dragon called Jasper, who no matter how hard he tries, doesn't fit in with the fire breathing dragons. But after putting out a house fire he's invited to join the Fire Brigade and he becomes Jasper the Fire Fighting Dragon. Once Jasper realises that he can put his talent to good use, and he stops trying (and failing) to be like the other dragons, things start going right for him. The moral of the story is that being different can be the very thing that makes someone special.

Thanks to social media the book was brought to the attention of groups for which I wouldn't have even thought of approaching. A foster care organisation said how great it would be for their foster parents to have copies of the book, to read to children who've had a tough time. Parents with autistic children asked if they could promote the book within their support groups as it gives a positive spin on being different. Teachers and parents have praised the anti-bullying aspect to the book. Stories of children's relationship with Jasper have started to filter back to me. One little boy said that he can relate with Jasper as he's picked on for being the only one with ginger hair. Another little girl talks about Jasper as if he were her friend. This little girl, called Ailla, requested a sequel in which Jasper gives a lion a shower! It completely warms my heart to hear that children (who are not related to me) actually enjoy the book.

When people hear that I published the book while on maternity leave they think that I'm absolutely bonkers – their words, not mine. But it's not as hard as everyone thinks. Everyone knows that new parents walk around in a sleepy daze because they are up at all hours with the baby. However this time can be utilized. When I was on maternity leave with Elizabeth, I devoured books; I went to Mummy-Zumba every Thursday; I staved off baby brain by taking Elizabeth around top London attractions and I met up with other yummy-mummies in cafés where we compared baby stories. I had a great time, but I was also learning how to be a mum and look after this precious little person. I wanted to be around other new parents, so we found reasons to meet up. Second time round, I didn't need the same level of support as I already knew about feeding routines, amber teething anklets, baby sign language, baby led weaning and all of the many, many other things that you suddenly learn about when you have a baby. However, with Imogen, I still had to spend hour upon hour feeding her throughout the day and night. Whilst breast feeding, you are basically sitting there, with free time on your hands. You can't clean, you can't cook, you can't do the shopping, you have to sit and let her feed. So, when did I work on promoting Jasper the Fire Fighting Dragon? While breast feeding my baby. I sat with my smart phone in my hand, and I talked about it in forums; came up with adverts to put on my Facebook page; wrote emails and articles about it. You name it, if I could do it on my phone whilst breastfeeding, then I did.

I also asked for a lot of help. I needed to learn how to make social media work for me. So I joined groups with names like 'Tech Angels', 'How to Build a Business Online', 'London Business Group', 'The Art of Making Profits From Your Purpose' and of course 'Mums In Business Association' to name but a few. These groups were enormously helpful and full of tips such as: when posting adopt the Four P's of Social Media:

Promotion (this is my book!)
Personal (I'm Val and this is my family)
Party (here's something that you're going to enjoy)
Professor (it's good for children to read)

I learnt that I had to engage with other users who either shared a target audience with me or who were my target audience. I discovered that I should react and reply to anyone who commented on my posts (it's only polite!) I looked at what was trending, posted videos, boosted posts, created adverts, got involved in engagement pods and found out as much as I could about algorithms – a word that months earlier hadn't been part of my vocabulary! There were countless occasions when I was chatting with people and had to be honest and tell them that I had no idea what they were talking about. Whenever I was asked about my metrics, my copy or my CTA, it just went over my head.

The frustrating thing is that marketing is essential if you want people to know about your business. After all, you can have the best product in the world, but if no one knows about it, then they can't buy it. There were so many occasions when I would turn to my husband and say 'but I'm good at writing. It's a good book, why isn't that enough?' At these moments, he would remind me that I enjoy telling people about the book. This is of course true and with this little moral boost I'd get back to my networking. I've also worked out that networking and marketing is basically just telling people about something that you like. I think of it as gossiping about my product: I'm telling a story. By switching my mindset from 'I don't know anything about marketing' to 'I've got a great story to tell you' everything became manageable and enjoyable. It was still trial and error. I tested out every theory that I came across and some things worked better than others. Of course, this all helped me when I went back to work. I was able to transfer my new social media knowledge to both Brit Movie Tours and Traditional Tours UK as well as Jasper the Fire Fighting Dragon.

Once my 6 months maternity leave finished, it was a lot harder to fit everything in around a full-time job and raising a family. So again I had to prioritise tasks and utilize any spare moment that I could find. How do you do this? Lists! They are amazing! Every time a job crept up, I emailed it to myself, then added it to my to-do list. I started doing a lot of work in the evenings after Elizabeth had gone to bed and Imogen was feeding. Despite this, sales dropped dramatically when I went back to work. What to do about it? In the words of Dory 'just keep swimming. Just keep swimming!'

What does the future hold for Jasper the Fire Fighting Dragon? Truthfully, I don't know. I hope that it continues to sell. I hope that Mum's will continue to buy it and children will continue to read it, but only time will tell. Secretly (or not so secretly) I would love Jasper the Firefighting Dragon to be the first book in the Jasper Dragon Series. I've already written a couple more adventures for Jasper. If I can get Jasper the Fire Fighting Dragon off the ground then I'd love to publish the others too. B ut I know that I've got to focus all my energy on this book first. If I want it to be around in 10 years, then I've just got to keep going. However if life takes over, if my priorities change and t he book stops selling, I'm incredibly glad that I took a risk and published it. My family and I will always treasure this book.

Hopefully it is clear that I love my book. I wouldn't put up with all the hassle of promoting it if I didn't! I'm going to finish by revisiting my initial thought: that I enjoy my work. If you don't really like doing whatever it is that you do, then ask yourself what do you enjoy? What are you good at? Now
work out how you can make money from that talent. Then ask yourself what's stopping you from giving it a go? Good luck.

# 16. VICKY LOUISE

I had a normal childhood we didn't have huge amounts of money but I had everything I needed. At the age of 8 my step sister dropped a HUGE bombshell, on the day my Mum and Dad got married she told me the dad I lived with wasn't my real Dad. I asked my Mum the next day if it was true and that's when they sat me down and told me about my biological Father and showed me a picture of him. I had not seen or heard from my biological Father since I was just over 1. I hadn't missed out because I had an amazing Step Dad who stepped up and took me on as his own. That aside questions would run through my head like why doesn't my Dad want me, why doesn't he contact me, what have I done wrong. It's a lot for a child to take in and I don't think it fully sunk in for a while. My mum asked me if I wanted my surname changed to my Step Dads surname and I agreed as far as I was concerned he was my dad. Life carried on and I was a typical mardy and moody teenager, I didn't like the fact I had to be in at 8.30pm at nearly 16. Me and my mum would constantly argue, at one point I ran away from home and I stayed with my nan for a while.

It was at 16 I also ended up with an eating disorder that I hid so well no one knew I told my mum a few years ago and she was shocked as she didn't have a clue. I would pretend I had eaten, I would tip crumbs out the toaster onto plates to make it look like I had eaten, I would survive for a long time just eating apples I was 5ft 9 inch and I weighed 8 stone I was ridiculously skinny. I was only when I met my boyfriend and he started forcing me to eat that I actually started eating and put some weight on. Things blew up when I had not long turned 16 after yet another argument I packed all my stuff and left home thinking I knew all about the world. The first night I stayed with a friend and after that I was put into a hostel, this hostel was mostly full of young lads into drugs and I had to share a toilet and bathroom with them. I was that scared I slept with a knife under my pillow as they were constantly knocking my door. My boyfriend at the time had moved house and it was only by pure fluke I remembered the new address, I spent my last money getting there and I got off at the wrong stop and had to walk the rest of the way in the pouring rain. I turned up there soaked to the bone and I stayed there for the night, I lied and told him and his Dad that the hostel was nice. Well when they took me back there they walked into my room and my boyfriend and his Dad wouldn't let me stay there and so I moved in with them. I missed the last 6 months of school whilst all this was going on my head of year promised me a bus pass as it was 2 buses to school and 2 buses back, well she let me down and my grades suffered massively. I sat 8 GCSE'S and I passed 7 with grades c to g and 1 ungraded, not the results I wanted at all. At the age of 17 I got engaged my Mum was not impressed one bit and our relationship was still very strained to say the least.

At 17 I also found out I was pregnant I went to a family planning clinic and they asked me to go back the next week and my pregnancy test was negative. I had had a miscarriage. Their reply to me was well you were pregnant but you're not anymore, this is something I kept to myself for a long time. Also at the age of 17 I decided to try and find my biological father, I found my auntie here quite quickly and she put me in touch with him. He was in western Australia and I found out I had 3 sisters over there as well as aunties and uncles there and here. I went over to Australia to meet him thinking I would get answers or the very least an explanation. Well I was in for a massive disappointment he hardly spoke to me his wife had more to say then him. I even went over another 2 more times after that with still the same no relationship not even conversation with him it was all hard work on my part and nothing back from him.

We started planning the wedding for me to get married at the age of 18 well actually xactly a week after my 18th. My Mum and Dad refused to come to the wedding and also wouldn't allow my little sister to come as they didn't want me to get married and didn't agree with it at all. This was one of the best and worst times of my life instead of me planning my wedding with my Mum I was doing it mostly on my own. I had a creative flare back then, I made my own bouquet, got already iced cakes from Tesco's and decorated them with flowers. The wedding came around and I was convinced my Mum would still come but she didn't this literally broke my heart. I wasn't given away by my Dad I was given away by a cousin I had only met the week before. Not long after we got married my husband became ill, a doctor diagnosed him with a stomach ulcer but with no further tests done. A few months later he had become so ill he couldn't stand he was being sick and he looked awful, we took him to a and e and was told by a nurse he would change his ulcer tablets and send him home. Luckily, he saw a doctor and that doctor admitted him and saved his life!! We left him there for the night and they said they would make a plan the next day, I got there the next day and he wasn't in his bed when I questioned the nurse as to where he was she said he had gone into theatre to have a camera put into his stomach and have a look. By this point I was furious. I was his wife and they hadn't bothered to ring me and let me know, 4 hours later he's still not back and I'm going out my mind by now. Finally, the surgeon comes to see us and they tell me he had in fact had Crohn's disease and had never had an ulcer he was misdiagnosed, and this massive error nearly killed him. The Crohn's had got so bad it had twisted 3 feet of his bowel and it was all infected and it was actually poisoning him, they had to remove 3 foot of his large bowel and they had to cut him the whole length of his stomach even round his belly button and they had stapled him back together. All of his family were convinced I would leave as I was only 18 and we had only been married for 3 months, but I didn't I stayed and looked after him.

I worked 2 jobs working shifts in the call centre and then working nights in the pub, he didn't work for several years after this. Even when he was better he still wouldn't work. I was working my arse off in the pub and he would sit the other side of the bar and drink what I made. In this time, we both ended up in serious debt he was spending money on credit cards faster than I could make it back. He ended up in over £45,000 worth of debt and I ended up with over £25,000 worth of debt, we both ended up being made bankrupt he wasn't bothered about it but this was a massive low point for me. We eventually moved out and were meant to be trying for a baby. I found out my Husband had been going on dating websites putting pictures of his actual bits on there. I also found messages he had been sending to other women when I was out asking them to come around, even when I printed them out and showed him he still tried to deny it. In the end enough was enough and I kicked him out we had been married for nearly 6 years and had been together for 8 years. I came home and he had been to my house and he had taken everything all he left me with was a bed and that was it!! He came in once when I was sleeping and left a wedding photo with till death do us part on which freaked me out. Then I find out he has taken an overdose because I left him. This next bit is actually unbelievable 5 days after this overdose he has moved in with someone else and he's engaged to her!!! Yet apparently this wasn't going on before I kicked him out.

A few months after this I start talking to someone I used to go to school with and we hit it off, I would say as corny as it sounds he whisked me off my feet. The downside he was in the army and was based in Northern Ireland, he had 2 little girls and I took to them and treated them no different to if they were my own. Long distance relationships are hard work going weeks without seeing each other, he was very paranoid and jealous because he had been cheated on before. Not long after we get together depression hits me hard. I've started the divorce proceedings and divorcees are not nice. I take my first overdose I've taken anything and everything to try and make everything in my head go away. I end up with a friend shoving her fingers down my throat to make me bring some of them back up. Doctors change my tablets and for a while I'm ok well I think I am, for a while.

My other half surprises me and proposes on New Years eve and I accept. I am excited and start planning a wedding I have chosen my dress, my cars, the venue I'm paying bits off the wedding and yet my other half is paying nothing. I put the wedding back a year and tell him if he isn't serious and doesn't start paying off the wedding then I will cancel the whole lot as after one divorce I am not getting married again if he isn't serious. Guess what happens, he continues to blow his money and not paying a thing off the wedding so I cancel the whole lot. I have paid my dress off so I have to go and pick up a dress I'm not going to wear, I was so upset because my Mum didn't come to my 1st wedding and wasn't involved but she helped me pick my dress and helped me plan and then it was all shattered. This puts a huge strain on the relationship as I am still so angry. Then the depression is that bad now that I literally stay in bed I don't cook, I don't clean if there's pots I put them in the bin and buy new ones because I can't even face washing up. Another argument with my other half on the phone whilst he's away because he's sick of me sounding miserable. You can't truly know what depression is like unless you've had it, he just didn't get it. This is where the second overdose comes in, my other half must have had some sort of idea that I was going to do it because after I have taken well in excess of 60 to 70 tablets he had rang the police and paramedics and I had to let them in or the police were going to kick the door in. I get taken to hospital and into resus. Now this is the bit no one tells you about. You get treated like absolute dirt when you've taken an overdose because it's self-inflicted. I ended up admitted and stay there the night and I had to be assessed by a psychiatrist. They decide I'm on the wrong tablets and they change them.

A year later my partner comes out the army, at first, it's all exciting but the army doesn't prepare them for coming out at all, it's like you sign off and they just don't care. They don't have loads of bills to pay and they just waste their money on crap. He had no clue of anything about life. He struggled with depression as well and 2 people with depression, living in the same house is explosive, there's arguments, moods, anger, resentment to name just a few. He couldn't hold down a job and I ended up paying all the rent. One day I've had enough and I tell him to go I come home and he's done what my ex-husband did he's cleared the house all I'm left with is my bed and the dog. I was beyond mad at this point, but eventually we sorted things out and got back together. We then had my son a couple of years later and it's the same he can't stay in one job, he had 10 jobs in just over a year. We ended up living separate and it was strained I was doing everything for George as well as working and running my Hand Crafted by Victoria xx business. I also managed to do my NVQ 2 in health and social care. At one point I was working 6 nights a week in a care home as well as running my business and hardly seeing my son. I end up losing my job due to ill health. I have arthritis in my shoulder and back, fibromyalgia, bulging discs in my back which push on the sciatic nerve in my leg. This is when I start really pushing my business and making more things.

Originally my business was handmade cards, but when cheap places like card factory open and you can get a card for 39p no one wants to pay for a handmade card. Then it turned to what I do now personalised gifts, memory boxes, decorated hairbrushes, baubles and now the added personalised t-shirts. Yet again I gave my biological father chance after chance when I had my son, not so much as a phone call from him after I had him. I hardly hear from him. It came to blows and ends up in a massive row because I said I would not have him in and out my sons life like he has to me. He told me he wasn't bothered because he had another grandchild on the way and he deleted and blocked me on Facebook. I haven't heard from him since but it's no loss to me as I have my Dad here and my son has his Grandad here too, it's not about who made us it's who has always been there.

In early 2017 my Grandad is coughing up blood, he has an emergency scan and they thought he either had a lung infection or he had cancer. He tries a course of antibiotics and he is still the same, he goes back to see the consultant and they confirm he has lung cancer his whole lung is covered in a dark shadow. After he goes to the cash machine with my sister and he tells her he has saved up enough money for his funeral so I think he knew all along. This amazing man was not our Grandad by blood but he took us on as his own and did everything a Grandad should do and more. They gave him 3 to 6 months to live, and because I was a carer in an end of life home I knew what was going to happen and when. This was my downfall I was so good at my job that I knew what different smells meant and I wished more than anything that I could erase the part of my brain that made me have the knowledge to know when people are going to die. This is when anxiety reared its ugly head, I sat watching him get weaker, loose more weight and be in pain, and become anxious and agitated. I watched my nan try her hardest to give him his wish to die at home she looked after him with us helping for weeks. She hardly slept and he was so agitated that he would snap at her even though he didn't mean it. The cancer nurse was shocking she hated the fact me and my sister were carers and we knew what he needed and when. One day he had 11 injections when someone on end of life has more than 3 injections in one day the syringe driver goes in but she was adamant he didn't need it. He was on permanent oxygen, he lost so much weight there was nothing to him. My nan finally told the nurse she needed help as he would sit on the edge of the bed at night for hours as he was too scared to lay down because he thought he would die. They couldn't get the carers in quick enough, made my nan feel bad for wanting to look after him as long as she was able. One day I went and I just knew that he wouldn't last another day. He started coughing and it was what we call the death rattle it's normally how they start coughing before they pass away. I called my sister and mum and he deteriorated so much he had the syringe driver put in he couldn't speak anymore, couldn't sit up on his own or stand. He was still agitated and we called the nurse out and she did all they could to make him comfortable. My Sister asked if we were going home as it was late and we both had little ones, and for some reason I just couldn't leave I don't know why I just had a feeling. My nan was asleep and we checked on my Grandad and he was breathing very fast we called the nurses out again and we woke Nan to say they would be coming she went toilet and as she was in there he stopped breathing. We shouted her quick and she came back and he started breathing again, he carried on stop starting breathing for what seemed like a lifetime just as we thought he was gone he would gasp again. I will never forget my Nans face when he finally passed away, it was like a part of her died with him, she was devastated and was begging him not to go. He's the first person I had ever seen die, it wasn't peaceful or comforting it was the most awful thing I had seen in my life. The good thing for my Grandad was that he died at home as he wished with us all holding his hand and sat with him.

After all this my anxiety is through the roof, I don't want to leave the house, crowds make me panic, the feeling of you think everyone is staring at you even when they're not, the not sleeping, panic attacks. I end up on a high dose of diazepam and even with this I don't sleep. I end up having my dose of antidepressant being put up twice so on triple the dose. I went to see him twice at the funeral home and he looked peaceful and like the Grandad Ken I remembered but even seeing him peaceful all I see for months after him passing is what he looked like when he passed away it's like a flashback that's always there. I could no longer be a carer I just couldn't face looking after anyone else who was going to be on end of life. This is when I decided he wouldn't have wanted me moping around or upset so I make the MASSIVE decision of going back to college, the thought of it petrifies me a class full of adults I don't know and then a placement full of children and adults I don't know. Well the first day was so hard but I did it!! I used my placement to work with children with physical and learning disabilities. Those children saved me from myself, they proved to me that no matter what their condition was they gave all they could to improve their work and even improve their mobility and they were so happy. I completed a level 3 Teaching Assistant qualification, which is the equivalent of A levels not bad for someone who got rubbish GCSE'S. As a newly qualified TA I thought I could go straight to work well I hit yet another brick wall, childcare costs!! The average wage for a teaching assistant is not enough to cover £1,000 a month in full time nursery fees. So instead of sitting on my bum I put everything I have into running my business I work round my nearly 3-year-old, some days I am doing 20 hour days.

In the last 2 months I have got a vinyl machine and I am making handmade personalised t-shirts. I design them myself, cut them, heat press them onto t-shirts, bags and hoodies. I have been lucky enough that I have had an old friend buy me a specialised sublimation printer which will open my business up to so much more like pictures on slate, pictures on cushions, t-shirts, photo mugs and so much more. He has helped me to get a tool that will ensure I do this as a full-time job now. I work long nights but it's all paying off and I will make a better life for me and my son. I juggle being a mum, with chores and my business, and my medical problems. Just because I don't have a 9 till 5 mundane job that I hate doesn't mean I don't work. A normal job I wouldn't work late into the early hours of the morning but I do something I love and I'm determined to make it to the top. I get constant remarks of I don't have a proper job, I don't do anything all day and why do I bother. The simple answer is because I am proving to my son that you can do anything you put your mind to, even with others trying to drag you down.

My past doesn't define who I am, it's just made me stronger and made me determined to be the best I can. I now have such a good relationship with my mum she was there to pick me up when I crumbled after my Grandad passed away and even now if my anxiety or depression is swallowing me she will buy me a cake and a coffee! She was the one to will me on when I said I couldn't do it anymore or she even gives me a kick up the bum when I need it. You only get one Mum and I may be biased but my mum is amazing!! She came out of the other end of domestic violence from my biological Father and she hasn't let this swallow her up, so that there is my inspiration my amazing Mum.

# 17. CHRISTINA

My name is Christina Georgiou I am thirty-four years old and have been married to my husband Andreas for eleven and a half years now and together we have three children, two boys Stavros who is nine years old, Kiriakos who is six years old and a girl (little diva) Penny who is three years old. I was born in Burton – Upon – Trent, UK but moved around a few times up and down the country since the age of five years old due to my parents' businesses up until 2000 where we settled in the West Midlands and still currently living.

I had a very strict upbringing and we were told to respect our elders, go to school and educate ourselves, not allowed a boyfriend until we got married (yeah right), we were never allowed to go out and play with friends. I am the second eldest out of five siblings. We had each other and between the four of us girls we helped raise my brother whilst my mother went to work. My father was very ambitious he moved over to the UK from Cyprus when he was just twenty-one years old and he married my mother at nineteen. He hardly knew a word of English, but went straight to work in something he had no clue in what to do and also no education behind him. But he was a worker and got stuck right in. He is the eldest son out of eleven siblings so he had to stop school and go help at home. My mother was born and bread in the West Midlands and her life was completely different to my fathers. She went to school, college and got educated. It was drummed into our heads time and time again when we were younger that we had to grow up, go to school, marry a Greek boy and be a good wife (yes, a bit like My Big Fat Greek Wedding the movie).

I loved going to school and throughout my school years I made friends quite easy. Out of all my sisters I think I was the chattiest one, always smiling (my nickname was smiler) and had something to say, I could speak to the wall and make friends with it. So when we moved schools always by the end of the first day I would know the whole class and it felt like I was there from day one.

My business background is in the fast food takeaway industry. I knew from a young age though I didn't want to work in the fish and chip shop. Although I was very friendly I was quite shy up until the age of fourteen years old. I always remember one Friday tea time the busiest time of the week, this little old lady ordered her food, I gave her change back and she stood in front of everyone and started to count it. I was so embarrassed I started to cry and that was it I never worked in the shop again. Ohh and have a phobia of working a cashier till. Growing up I always knew I wanted to help people at first, I wanted to become a nurse, then work in a post office (I had the best post office set one Christmas from "santa") then I wanted to become a chef and own a hotel with a fab restaurant. I did quite well in my GCSEs they got me into college anyway. I then went on to do an Ilex Legal Secretarial Course, which I loved especially when my work placement was in the local police station. I was then offered a job with them for two weeks after I had impressed them with my office skills. One afternoon I went to the placement and all four staff had fallen ill (or so they say) and I had to run the office all by myself. Let's just say I did S**t myself. I always remember a phone call from a young lady she phoned up to say she wasn't going to sworn in and decided she didn't want to become a police officer anymore. I was seventeen years old at the time and I remember her crying her eyes out saying her boyfriend didn't want her to do it. I asked her "how do you feel, what is it you want out of your life?" do what makes you happy, if your boyfriend leaves then he isn't the one, he should stand by your decision and let you do what your passionate about, because why would you go for it in the beginning if you're not 100% right? After I put the phone down and reported it to the manager, I was thinking in my head "oh no what have I done, did I tell her the right thing, Shit I am going to get kicked out of my placement" but they were really impressed with how I dealt with it and that's when I go the job. Today I know now why having the right mind-set is the key to everything. My issue was I didn't believe in myself, I didn't have the mindset I have today because it was very rare and unheard of what we learn and practice today back then.

After I left college I was promised a job at the police station but it wasn't going to be available until the November of 2002. Well I left college in the July and I was bored and needed to get a job. My father needed help in the family business. We had sold the fish and chip shop and we are now in the food manufacturing industry. I take my hat off to my father.

No education behind him, barely read English but established a new business venture from the storeroom in the back of the fish and chip shop over thirty years ago. So I went to work with him and my first wage pack I was like WOW this is all mine. I am an eighteen-year-old girl with first wage package what do I do now? Yep off to the shops and I went and purchased my first designer bag, I still have it to give to my daughter and to tell her the story. I worked full time and stood by my father through the fun times and also the hard times, because let's face it business is never straight right? When I got married in 2006 to my husband he also is in the fish and chip shop trade and also into the property management industry. It was expected of me to leave my father's business and go and work with my husband in the chippy. I didn't want to and I said to my husband I am not coming to work with you. I have a job I love and I am not shifting. We purchased our first business together I helped him out for a couple of weeks then went back to my job, I think it was because I was comfortable and I didn't like the change in my work.

Five years ago was the hardest time of my marriage. My husband fell into depression and was having anxiety attacks for a while which led us to separate for six months and I moved back in with my parents with my two boys at the time. It was really hard and frustrating, plus it was just painful to see my eldest suffering the way he was as he was very close with his dad. At that point in my life I had to become responsible and that's when I decided to set up my own business. It was an online children's wear boutique specialising in Orthodox Christenings. My husband and I decided to try again because we couldn't bear seeing Stavros the way he was. It was hard but we pulled through it and I am happy that we did. We both come very different backgrounds, so it was very hard to adapt to each other but we pulled through it. As children, it was drummed into the guy's head that the "wife" should stay home, cook, clean and look after the children while the men go out to work. This was a big issue for his family especially his father that I didn't want to be at home and be a typical "housewife". We then found out that I was almost three months pregnant with Penny.

I have always tried doing something alongside my full-time job. I just wanted to have something of my own. I am not afraid of working; I tried network-marketing years back with a company that shut down due to lack of funds. But I didn't get it, I never grew a team but I could sell ice to an Eskimo. I think it was because I was the youngest in the team and didn't have the experience I do now.

So this leads me to where I am today with my life and business, because I decided to do something for ME. I decided to get back my own identity as a woman and not just as a wife or a mother, but as Christina. I was on maternity leave with Penny and we had decided with my husband that I wasn't going to go back to work full time and stay home with the children. I had worked full time through my first two babies, I wasn't planning on missing out on this one. I had to get sterilised and so I wanted to enjoy every single second I could with my daughter.

At the age of 30 I had three children, two were in full time school and I had a newborn. I was bored, fed up and just couldn't handle being a "lady of leisure" so to speak. I had gone from full time work to nothing and I felt lost and not my independent self. After having my third c - section I wasn't well for the first six months had an operation and then my beauty business came into my life and it changed me as a person in so many ways, it was what was missing. I became my happy bubbly self again, so many inspiring women surrounded me and I was in my happy place, meeting new people is definitely something that I love.

My boys have a busy after school schedule, so Monday through to Sunday they have something on. It's been a hard year this year as my eldest is training to take his black belt in karate at the beginning of December. We have had to sacrifice family events etc so that he can get the training he needs as they fall on either a Saturday or Sunday. I find my slow cooker is my best friend especially through the week. I chuck whatever in and just switch it on at 8.30am so it's ready for them when we get home from school, then its straight back out the door. On Mondays its Greek School, Tuesdays is Karate, Wednesdays is Swimming, Thursdays is Violin for Kiriakos and Football for Stavros, Friday – Sunday is yep... FOOTBALL. God help me when Penny starts... She is already asking for ballet lessons again. Now that Penny is at nursery three times a week it does help me get a lot of house work done and also to get back on top of my business when I need to. All I can say is you need to plan, plan, plan. There are days I don't stick to it and boy don't I know it. My whole day can just go crazy then I'm running around like a crazy women trying to get back on track.. ohhhh and I am always late, yes I am one of those moms that turn up late to everything. But the beauty of all these activities is I get to meet new mums every day. I get asked every single day "How do you do it all?" well there are days where I don't even know how I do it, the beauty of working from home is that it just fits in around my day to day life and being on the go most days working from my phone is perfect.

When I signed up to my new business venture I didn't really think much of it and I got into something that was very out of my comfort zone but just went with it. I had people laughing at me and every time they would see me make a joke out of one of my videos that they came across. I developed a team within my first ten days and promoted twice within the first two months. I was buzzing and thought to myself wow I can finally do this. I signed up at the end of July 2015 and by the Christmas I had lost all ten of the ladies that had come on board. I took it quite bad and decided that I wasn't good enough for this. All that confidence that I had built had just gone within seconds. I doubted myself and really felt negative towards it all that I was thinking of packing it all in. Until I was speaking with the therapist when I was doing a course of body talk, a holistic therapy. She told me that I didn't have much willpower and that I may have inherited it from my Great Grandfather. Well that stuck in my mind and at that point I was ready to give up and I talked myself into to the fact that I wasn't good enough, even though the girls around me told me I was doing ok, I remembered what the therapist had said and I didn't give up. I was trying to figure a way to get me back on track, which

I then found that Instagram had helped me do this. So I re-launched my business back in March 2016. From that day, I didn't look back I just went for it, I had new ladies coming on board and I was promoting. I was so happy to be back to me again. I was asked to speak at a training event on how I built my business on Instagram. I travelled to Las Vegas on my own without any family or KIDS wow that felt strange. But I finally got my independence back and I just felt I was free again. Now doors are opening that I'd never imagined would. I am so grateful for everything in my life today. My business is growing and my confidence is growing in the sense that I can help women make a difference, if I can inspire someone to make a change then that's my job done.

When I joined the MIBA group, I was welcomed very quickly by Estelle. I was asked to speak to the group about what had worked for my business, it was such a pleasure to do and I was truly humbled. There are days that I do struggle to work especially with three young children all under the age of nine years old. But all I have to do is pop into the MIBA group and there's always someone who can help pick you up just by a post they may have posted on the struggles of their day, we can relate to one another and it's just fab. I truly feel I have found my home with in MIBA I can finally do what I have always wanted to do and that's to help people. If one post or quote can help make someone's day just that little bit better then I will keep going until they are in the place they truly deserve to be in their lives. We all have goals and dreams that we want to achieve in life, depending on how much you want them to become a reality is down to you. Believe that you already have and with hard work and determination you will receive. I never used to think much about the Universe or believed that God could make things happen. But if you don't ask you don't receive and believing that the Universe or God will give you what you want, is just how strong your thoughts truly are. I've seen lives change right before my eyes, because they believed in something so much that they got what they wanted plus they wanted their lives to change for the better. It is so easy to get into a rut and just keep going for the hell of it. As mothers and wives we lose ourselves and stop looking after our mind and body because we are so focused on looking after others. We deserve whatever we work for just as much as the next person. I am so grateful that I get to spend time with my family, get them involved in my business and work it from anywhere I like. MY WHY, my goals are to get back my family freedom, my husband has not had a day off over the past five years and I couldn't remember the last time we spent a weekend as a family together. Now things have started to change because I believe in that goal so much, it's happening. We want to travel the world, take the kids to see and learn about different cultures. I want them to be able to have a choice in life and do what will make them happy and not what's expected of us, go to school, college and University then get a nine 'til five job. Of course I want them to educate themselves. But I want them to go out that have the freedom they truly deserve.

So ladies all there is left for me to say, Stand strong, believe in yourselves and go chase those dreams... We have one shot at this... LIFE!! Go and enjoy it. xx

# 18. VICKY B

When my dad passed away my life as I knew it fell apart. I distanced myself from my mum and brother, lost my job and had what I can only describe as my 'Sex, drugs and rock and roll' years. I fell into a huge depression, a depression that told me constantly that I wasn't good enough, that I would never be good enough and that my family were ashamed of me.

After sitting in this deep dark depression for far too long I decided enough was enough, and made the promise to myself to sort my life out. I enrolled in college as a 'mature' student (I was only 22!) to retrain as a beauty therapist. I thought that if I was going to retrain in anything I needed to make it something that means you'll get something back and that something back was being practised on for facials, massages the lot, it was exactly what I needed.

At the end of my college course I gained a position to go and work on cruise ships, I had a few months to sell all my belongings, give up my flat and say goodbye to sunny Devon. It felt good to be leaving a place that had seen me through my worst, it felt like a new start and that I was finally doing something that people would be proud of.

When I had been interviewed by the cruise ship company they had noticed two small tattoos I had on my wrists, they were of mine and my dad's initials. I had been inked with them not long after my dad's passing and they meant a lot to me. They had explained to me that tattoos were not allowed to be visible whilst I was working and that I needed to do something about them. Unfortunately, back then in 2004 laser tattoo removal treatment was new and hugely expensive, being a student all I could afford was to have them removed with acid. Every week I would have a wrist worked on, where they would get a tattoo gun, dip it in acid and then push down into my tattoo, move it up by a teeny tiny bit and then push down again. This meant the acid would supposedly be beneath the ink and would push it out to the surface into the scab and then come off. It was horrifically painful but I continued on and on right up until the week before I was due to leave for the academy.

My tattoos were still visible but only as a dull grey outline when I arrived at the academy. I had also purchased some pretty expensive tattoo cover up make up that was suitable for massage therapists to wear as it was waterproof and anti-allergenic etc., I felt confident that I would make it through with this and would soon be on a ship massaging my way around the world. It wasn't to be, on my second day at the academy I was hauled into the office and questioned about my tattoos. They made me sit there and unpick the tattoo removal stuff I had expertly applied to show them what was there, and was subsequently kicked out of the academy and the hostel we were staying in on the spot.

To say I was devastated was an understatement.

I went back to the hostel packed up my tiny suitcase and left, not knowing anything about London or a single person. Every time I had ever travelled to London from Devon I had always landed into Paddington by train so this was where I headed, it was the only familiar place to me. Once there I booked myself into a bed and breakfast to work out what I was going to do.

I didn't call anyone, I couldn't bear to call anyone and tell them that yet again I had failed. I also didn't want to go back home. I had said my goodbyes to everyone, I had had an 'I'm leaving' party, I couldn't go back home with my tail between my legs.

I had enough money to stay in the B&B for a week, so I told myself I would give myself this time to work out what I wanted to do. During the week, I popped into a pub I had visited on previous trips to London, again a pub that felt familiar and safe. One night I got talking to the landlord and he was in need of staff, I suggested that if he could give me somewhere to stay I would work in the pub for a reduced wage whilst I worked out what I wanted to do.

Now I was earning (albeit a small amount) and had a roof over my head I had the space to work out what it was that I wanted to do. I knew I didn't want to go back home but I knew I had to get something sorted.

I ended up calling the manager of the company I worked for part time whilst retraining as a beauty therapist and he managed to find me a job in the city for the same company. I was so grateful for this and it led to the most amazing 10 years in London. I ran a concession in Harrods and launched a shop in Westfield, earnt enough to have my own rented flat in Shepherds Bush - No sharing of bathrooms or having to wash up other people's plates before I could cook myself, my own place! It was amazing. I also met my husband and gained a management position for one of the largest companies in the world.

Things were bumbling along great, life was pretty amazing and then I got pregnant, it was totally planned but what caught me off guard was the fact that I was petrified of childbirth. Every time I thought about giving birth I cried. Instead of burying my head in the sand I did what I always do, I headed to the internet to find out how I could do to get over this.

This is where I stumbled across Hypnobirthing, Doulas and Placenta Encapsulation. You see, on top of being petrified of giving birth I was even more terrified of developing post-natal depression. As I had suffered depression previously I was a higher risk of developing it again. Keeping on top of my depression is something that I have to work on daily, I have to make sure I check in with myself and look after myself to stop the deep black hole from swallowing me again. I couldn't bear the thought of going back there. All three of these things hypnobirthing, placenta encapsulation and having a doula would all help me birth my child and help me prevent post-natal depression.

I booked all 3 and they totally changed my world. The hypnobirthing took me from someone who was shaking and crying every time I thought of giving birth to someone who smiled when her waters broke and I look back on giving birth so fondly. In fact, I bloody love giving birth and would happily give birth any day of the week.

My doula helped guide me and my husband through our labour and supported up when a curve ball was thrown in and helped us make the decisions that we needed to make.
And the placenta encapsulation, well those little beauties are like red bull in capsule form. I don't even remember having the baby blues they were that amazing.

I knew after having some honest conversations with my manager at work before going on maternity leave that I wouldn't be offered a part time position after my leave was up, so I decided to retrain again. This time I retrained to be a teacher of The Wise Hippo birthing programme, the programme I had used in the run up to giving birth and a placenta encapsulator.

Both those things totally changed my world and I have never looked back.

Being able to help guide a pregnant couple through their journey to birth is a truly wonderful thing, as is getting those emails from clients telling me that they did it, that they had a birth that they were in control of, that they felt empowered throughout and one that they look back on with pride whether they had a natural birth, a C-section or a birth that involved every drug going. You see I don't care how my clients give birth, they can give birth at home, in hospital or in a forest surrounded by goats. I really don't care. What I care about is that they have a birth that they can look back on and know that every decision they made was theirs and that when they settle into family life they have absolutely no questions about their birthing journey because they felt empowered enough to ask the medical professionals about every step they went through during their birth.

And then the placenta encapsulation service I offered, just knowing I was able to help women post-natal journey smoother as amazing.

I worked as a placenta encapsulator for 3 years, building my business up to the point that I was turning people away.

I felt hugely proud of myself that yet again I had managed to again rise from nothing, I had created a business that was successful and turning a profit. Being able to work the hours I wanted to and able to fit the business around my husband who works away a lot and spend time with my little one was such a huge thing to me, I was able to deliver my Wise Hippo classes and process placentas whilst my little man was sleeping so he had a full-time mummy as well as a mum to be proud of.

It was when I got pregnant with my second child that I realised my life and business was going to have to be overhauled again. My husband was working away for even longer periods of time and I soon realised that I wouldn't be able to work as I had been now that I was soon to be juggling two little ones. It was tiring enough with the one child, but I just knew that when I had two little ones I wouldn't have the energy to go out of an evening and work whilst they slept and be a great mum the next day. I knew something had to give, in the past year I had totally burnt myself out a couple of times and had to take a break so I knew things couldn't continue as they were.

The placenta encapsulation part of my business was what took up the most amount of my time, and also it was far too unpredictable to do whilst having a baby and a toddler. Babies come as and when they want too and the drop everything and dash to a hospital to collect a placenta was not going to be easy with two children. So the decision to drop this service from my business was made, but I had no idea as yet what to fill it with. I needed something that I could continue to bring in money with, without leaving the house. With my husband away for weeks at a time at some points of the year the thought of arranging childcare etc. for a service that took me away from the house filled me with dread.

It was weeks and weeks later at a business conference that I had booked to go on before I was pregnant that the idea popped into my head.

Having worked in the birth and baby industry for a while now I had not only made a lot of friends in the same line of work but I had also became increasingly frustrated with the huge costs of getting your business out there.

So I created a website and Facebook page that would advertise the birth, baby and child businesses throughout Suffolk at a ridiculously reasonable cost. Not only that but the business would give back, give back to people in need both globally and locally.

Whilst at the business conference I had come across this amazing business called B1G1 (Buy 1 give 1) and instantly become a premium partner. This meant that I could give a percentage of any money that came into the business to help causes throughout the world, it felt great to know that my teeny tiny little business could make a difference in someone else's life.
Not only that I wanted to make sure that we gave back locally too. As a Wise Hippo birthing teacher, I had offered my services to help the pregnant women who were in our local refuges.

These women are quite often moved miles away from friends and family for their safely and often can't tell anyone where they are and therefore face giving birth alone.

When someone they loved had taken away their control etc. I wanted to go in and give them all the tools and techniques they would need to be in control during birth. That they would feel empowered and safe knowing that they could do it, they could give birth alone and feel safe.

I wanted to continue to help these women so I have also gone on to create a fund to help support these women, a percentage of any money that comes into the business gets put aside ready to pay a fellow hypnobirth teacher to go and teach (at a reduced rate) these women how to birth confidently and stay in control as and when we get a call to say they have someone in their unit.

When I launched this second business I was 38 weeks pregnant with my second child, she is 1 in a couple of weeks and I cannot begin to tell you how proud of myself I am for working hard enough to get it off the ground and to make it a success. Knowing that not only am I bringing money into the house but the fact that the business helps support people in need globally and locally. I have grand plans for The Baby Experts Suffolk and can't wait to see where the next few years take me.

When I look back to where I was 14 years ago when my dad passed away and the journey I have been on in those years I see one pattern emerging, again and again.

When the sh*t hits the fan, don't let it floor you. Step away, take the time and work out what that next step is, be kind to yourself and don't beat yourself up. Don't wallow in the self-pity and negativity that will not get you nowhere and always look to change everything into a positive.

So many people disowned me during my 'sex, drugs and rock and roll' years when all I needed was a good hug, my hand held and looking after, and I'm sure when people read this and learn of the fact I attempted to take my own life not once but twice they will look at me differently but you know what, I don't care. What I care about is my family, I care that they are well looked after. That they have a mum that's there to pick them up from school, to clean up their sick and to run around like loons in the park together.

I care that my kids grow up knowing that they can be whatever they want to be as long as they put the work in. I want them to follow their dreams and do something that makes their hearts beat with joy and not get stuck in a job that fills them with dread.

I care that my closest friends think I'm a grounded down to

earth person who works hard to achieve her dreams.

And I also care that anyone around me, no matter even if I've only met them once, that if they are going through a tough time with depression, anxiety anything like that, that I will be there for them. I will be that truly un-judgmental person that they can have a cup of tea with and chat about whatever they need to chat about in that moment, because I've been there.
I know what it feels like to think that your nearest and dearest will judge you for having depression, to be scared to open up and stand there and say hey this is me and I'm going through a tough time at the moment and I need your support. I will always be there for you.

# 19. SANDIE

My name is Sandie, I am 24 years old and have 3 beautiful children and I am happily Married! Now we have the boring part out the way, I'm going to be giving you a little insight to my Journey and how I became a mumpreneur!

The reason I am sharing my story is not because I want any sort of limelight but because I come across woman everyday who feels that they are not worthy enough of success or that they don't fit some kind of criteria!

This saddens me greatly and that's why I love my new-found career as a professional network marketer! Because literally ANYBODY can do it!

So a few people laugh and joke about me and say I could write a book about my life and what I have achieved because I have come across some real hurdles in life!

I am not your typical business woman or at least the typical business woman that the media likes to make out.
I have had a very rough start in life and found myself within the care system quite young. I often got told and heard people say that it's game over once you end up in the viscous cycle of moving from foster home to foster home, surrounding yourself with what people would call "disturbed and neglected kids".

I wasn't quite sure whether I wanted to go into detail about what I had actually been through as I am sure you can appreciate it can bring back some very dark and painful memories! In fact, my first version of my story was quite basic, but I really wanted to connect with people who have perhaps been in the same situation as myself and feel there is no way out!

So here goes!

From as young as I can remember I never had a connection with my mum, some people may read this and think WHAT? But yes, it's true there wasn't a connection as what I now realise should be there. I have a younger sibling too who this doesn't effect and I have never been the one to hate on her because of this. I try and understand but I can't put the pieces together and I don't think I ever will. My mum was very poorly just after she had my sister with Cancer and my Nan looked after us a lot. SO maybe this is the reason why!? I don't know.

My Dad? He left when my sister was young and created a new life with his wife and they felt that it wouldn't be suitable for me to ever live with them.

When I was 6 years old my mum threw me out. Literally. She left me at the side of the road and asked my nan to come and collect me because she couldn't handle it anymore. So off I went and lived with my Nan. She is a truly amazing lady! I spent the past 7 years in her care, now I'm not going to lie I wasn't the easiest child and my behavior was getting worst and worst. I basically did what I wanted, when I wanted with whom I wanted. Looking back now I put myself in situations where I am lucky to still be here! I also suffered years of constant bullying this may also have an effect on why I had the "don't give a shit approach". and things soon started to become dark! I was with the wrong crowds constantly and at just 11-12 years old I found myself in a position one evening where there were a few friends who had met a few boys of a on a park. We were drinking and having a laugh. This was not the first time we had done this but the first time with these boys/men. Before I knew it I woke up the next morning getting ready for school as if everything was normal. I have never heard my Nan scream so much in her life when I strolled in the kitchen!

Little did I know that the night before I had been picked up by the police as they had seen me via CCTV crawling along the market in the small town where we had moved too. Luckily, they knew my nan and brought me home. I had no idea and couldn't remember any of this; it was clear, and my Nan and the police knew I had been spiked......but it was something they couldn't prove!

It was at this point when my nana told me the full details of what happened the night before.........when I got home I couldn't move, I had my pants down to my ankles and was covered in mud. My nan and grandad had to carry me into the bath to wash me down!

How could this be? How can I not remember? The police came the next day to take statements and also provided us with the info that another girl was found close to me in the same state and if I knew her. I didn't and I'd never seen her in my life.
So they gave me a drunken disorderly fine!? CRAZY EH? Looking back now, I can't believe that at the age of 12, I was known to the police and getting treated like a criminal when I was the victim.

The next few days I went back into school and started to re-connect with the people I was with (friends) and I was mortified......someone had videoed that night and the video was circulating around the village of me with a group of men! I don't really need to go into detail much more as I'm sure you can guess!

MY LIFE AT THIS POINT WAS OVER! I was so humiliated and angry but for the wrong reasons!

I was getting flashbacks from the night; I was young, the police didn't care and who would believe the out of control teenager! I couldn't bring myself to go back in or go out. I was angry and my behavior spiraled out of control. My Nan couldn't cope which I don't blame her for.

This is when I took my first overdose, at the age of 12! Looking back now, I realise it was a huge cry for help, at such a young age I had no way out.

I was rushed into hospital and luckily, I hadn't done much damage I remember a psych coming to see me and asking all different kinds of questions which I wasn't bothered about I just wanted to get out the place.

My Nan decided it would be best that I went back to my mum. So off I go back to Blackpool where it was made quite clearly, I wasn't welcome there. In fact, it lasted a whole of 3 weeks. I had a new school and had new friends. I managed to find myself in the "popular" group. GREAT! How wrong was I! It was a group of girls and boys being completely brainwashed and followed a girl who in my eyes is pure evil! She manipulated every single person in this group even at school the teachers wouldn't say boo too her! Makes me sick to my stomach thinking back. I got attacked regularly in the cruelest ways and so did others. The control from this so-called human being was that bad she would tell us when we were to go out, what times, where to meet and what we wore! Crazy! I remember sitting in an alley with a piece of glass self-harming all because of the control and too scared to not do what she ordered, or if she had tricked me again leading me to have 6 people jumping on my head.

I became quite close to one of the other girls and their mum and when my mum kicked me out after 3 weeks she allowed me to live with them.

I am so grateful to them even now, however as I'm sure you can appreciate that didn't last long. It wasn't their responsibility. So off I go back to my mums – it lasted another week or two. In the meantime, I met a guy and started living with him and his family. Again, still very young and very stupid he was a lot older than me and it didn't last very long. I then met another guy through friends and ended up staying regularly at their house. I went back to my mums and she would not let me in! I needed some stuff, she accused me of stealing a large amount of money and I remember staying outside her house for 5 hours not even being allowed to use the bathroom! My sister and my mum throwing my belongings out the windows.......at the age of 13.

I went into school the next day and reported that I had nowhere to go! The end of school came and somebody from the office had called me into a room, this was weird! Waiting there for me was a social worker ready to take me to my new home. What? Now this is not normal and to this day it makes me well up, the fear!

I remember this social worker taking me to my mums collecting my things, she was there and said nothing. And that was it........off I go!

I walked into this strange house and a lady called "Stella" appeared she was quite old and had a husband and loads of dogs.

She reminded me of a witch. Very set in her ways. I went into my new bedroom and remember lying there all night just crying, petrified knowing that this is just not normal!

I am living with people who are getting paid to have me there! I am a CHILD!

Turns out this "witch" soon put me in my place and gave me stability and taught me things I never knew existed. In the meantime, I still had my boyfriend who conveniently lived 2 streets down.

Things was going good, well as good as things could possibly be. Until I realised I had not had a period that month so I took myself to the doctors and there it was that second little line appeared. 14 and PREGNANT!

I was petrified and I knew Stella would be so disappointed, I was in care what would happen?

There was no way about it, I was keeping my baby.......this is where I realised something had to change! This was the turning point of my life!

I decided that I needed an education and I needed grades, I had to give my baby the best start in life! I had to have goals! Unfortunately, I had to move foster homes as Stella couldn't provide for both me and the baby, so when I was 37 weeks pregnant I moved to another home which didn't last very long. So I got to work and when my boy was 6 months old I passed my GCSE's. Went on to Passing my A levels! I came out the care system at 16 with my baby! And fought hard for him not be in the system when I was!

Things didn't work out between myself and baby's dad! Which

is understandable I was too young to know what a relationship was. So I cracked on, on my own.

Whilst studying I re met with an old school friend and we hit it off! He seemed great! My age, he had a son, amazing!

However, things started turning bad pretty quickly! I suffered beatings numerous times and shortly after I gave birth to my second child I had an extremely lucky escape. He is now in jail for stabbing a lady after watching her granddaughter in a dance show! I need say no more.

So after the shocking news and having a 2 week old baby I began to feel helpless and low again! However, I thought to myself I've done this on my own before I can do it again! I decided to go for it and got myself into UNI!

Amazingly, I picked myself back up and shortly after I met a great guy. I don't know how it happened it just did. After a whirlwind romance, we got engaged to be married. I was so happy I had found someone however I couldn't quite believe I was good enough for him all due to my past relationships. It was 2 weeks before my wedding and I had a bit of a break-down where I felt I couldn't cope anymore. Not many people know about this but I was constantly getting flashbacks of what happened at the park that night, it was all coming back, that and the fear of losing someone else who I loved and I decided this is it....It's over!

I took so many tramadol's and co-codamols, how I am still alive today I do not know!

The thought of being weak and things going wrong again scared the living day lights out of me!

I ended up being ok JUST! And I didn't realise how amazing my future was looking! I was lucky! Very lucky!

I had a new lease of life. I managed to land my dream job within health and social care sector and was loving life! Don't get me wrong we didn't have the perfect start but we fought through it. I now have 3 amazing children and a Husband!

Reflecting back, throughout my whole life I have been let down by those who I trusted and loved. I was just a little girl, like any other, who craved love and attention and it backfired. All these years of low self-esteem, going through the care system and I've come out the other side. It could have been so different.... I feel like a cat who has 9 lives! Now with gorgeous children, a husband and I've even built bridges with my family. What's the point in holding grudges, life is too short and precious.

Another new chapter had begun for me, although I had a dream job on the outside, on the inside it wasn't fulfilling me anymore. Working long unsociable hours, no work/life balance or recognition for the hard work that I put in, I knew that there must be something more. If I could do what I have done already after what I have been through, surely, I could do anything?

I had the idea in my head that I had to make it happen! It was on obsession. I felt like I had to prove to everyone what I could do.

I had little to no work life balance and I was beginning to hate my much-loved career. What could I do? How would I solve this? At the time I was on a very good Salary and I couldn't see a way out! How could I do this without jeopardising a pay cut? I simply couldn't do because I was the breadwinner.

Something clicked and I remember a girl popping up on my Facebook news feed a couple of years ago and had noticed how amazing her life was, she had a business, always with the kids, new car, kids in private school and was travelling for free! I was curious and if I'm honest I envied her life!

So instead of sitting back watching her I decided to bite the bullet and approach her to ask her what it was she was actually doing! I was sick of just watching.

I am so thankful and I believe that god has rewarded me for being patient and holding on! What network marketing has done for me in such a short space of time if just incredible!

I don't often tell my story, in fact I've never really have and ff I do, I like to miss out the majority of it. Even though I had a great job already and I had fought so hard to get there I could see something in my network marketing company that nothing has ever been able to give me! Time, money, freedom and self-development.

Don't get me wrong I did question myself a few times whether I was the perfect fit for the whole business woman thing, but I soon got over it. Why not me? My past is my past and it has made me the person I am today!

I fought so hard to be able to believe in myself and even look in the mirror without feeling sick!

We all have our reasons "WHY" within our businesses and this is the most important part. When I first started out my "WHY" was my children but this soon changed! I dug a little deeper and my "WHY" is to help women all over the world. Women who feel they are not worthy of success or have no self-esteem! I was once that girl in the corner thinking I didn't deserve to be on this planet! Times can still be tough, I'm only human, but I know the future is a lot brighter and I'm really excited for what is to come.

I now know you can be anything you ever wanted to be! You just have to believe in yourself! Anything is possible.

I now take my past and use it as my staircase to success. My experiences have made me who I am today, I use this as an advantage not a disadvantage.

I am now 7 months into my network marketing business and MY GOD! Apart from giving birth to my children it is BY FAR the best thing I have ever, ever DONE!

It's still very early days for me however what I have achieved so far, I am so proud of! But the best part is KNOWING and BELIEVING in what I can do and what I can do to help others that have been in a similar situation to me.

I am still a normal person, down to earth and I will never change as a person. I will never forget my past but it no longer haunts me.

The most successful people are the ones that had nothing! The ones that have been through hell and back! The ones that are still here today telling their stories on how people like myself and like many other people all over the globe didn't GIVE UP! From that girl who had no hope! Being dragged around the care system, being abused, bullied and getting pregnant very young, to the girl who never gave up and has found her place where nobody can stop her and making her children very proud every single day.

Rock bottom has built more champions than privilege ever did!

# 20. MYISHA

Whether you're a Thriving Single MOM-preneur, Busy MOM-preneur or MOM-preneur in action, you realize that your identity is intersectional. Your role as a mother comes first and plays a huge part in how you manage your day to day life as business owner.

Early in my life, there was never a time in I don't remember seeing my single mother not struggling to take care of her children. My mother worked hard and while I felt I was missing out on her presence, it was her "doing what she has to do." Work 8-12 hours per day to provide for myself and my brother. When she had time, she could come to events, and to the school, but I wanted more than she can give. It was only her. From that experience, I knew at an early age that I didn't want to work the 9-5, I wanted to be the next "Oprah" to hopefully be more present in the lives of my children and I would do anything I had to, to make sure I could. As children, we all dream of what we want to be, but who would have thought I would've ended up living my intention that I set at a young age?

Now as a full time MOM-preneur I know what it's like to "do what I have to do." Like my mother, I too am a single mother of three different-abilities children. Let's just say that I now know and I understand the anger, frustration, and stress of parenting AND running a business full time.

My intention for writing this story is to leave YOU empowered to know that you can survive heartache, loss, mental illness AND overcome to thrive as an amazing MOM-preneur.

Within the last 18 years of my life I have lost more of myself in the physical world, but spiritually have gained a deeper awareness in who I really am and whom I serve. 1 mental health hospitalization, 6 pregnancies, and 3 amazing children later, I realize this is the path that lead me to becoming the MOM-preneur I am today. You may notice I say tend to capitalize the MOM in "preneur", I do this to emphasize that as a business owner, my family takes priority and my business has to work around the lives of my children.

I had my first pregnancy at 18 4 months later I found out my baby's heart didn't beat and was scheduled for a D&C. Nearly 2 weeks later, the baby passed on its own. At the time, I never grieved the loss and I went through a depressive stage and sat in my room for a month or so and just zoned out. What helped bring me out of this state was my full-time job at the Home Depot. I thought life waa good until I became a victim of physical and emotional abuse.. I lived with my abuser for 2.5 years within that same period, I became pregnant (not by my abuser) two more times and lost two more babies within 12 months of each other. Talk about a hard blow. Doctors told me I'd never have children again, as there may be something wrong with my uterus' ability to carry children. Imagine being 20 and losing 3 children within a 3-4-year time span. Thus, began a 3-year period of hopelessness with nowhere to turn.

How does one recover after such loss? Well I was young and naive and learned to bury it with alcohol. Somewhere in this dark spiral of alcohol addiction, I found hope with my godsisters and adoptive family who took me in and helped point my life in the right direction. Around this time, I fell in love with "the one." You know, the prince in shining armor that saves you from dark despair? It was all seemingly too good to be true. We, too, tried to have a baby and it was during this time I found out that I had HPV; further biopsy found that I had cancerous cells on my cervix that had to be removed. At 21, I found myself in a cycle of grief, but luckily, I had an amazing support team and the procedure went well. It was then when another doctor told me I could not bear children. It was hard to take, but I had my partner and my family. I knew it would be ok--or so I thought.

Fast forward a year and I find myself wanting to commit suicide as I was left by my partner. His sister was the one who help me find hope from that dark place. Left depressed and broken-hearted I had no choice but to go back home to my mother. Once I got to my mom's house, I felt frequent urges to visit my old friends and family. It seems lighthearted of sorts. But visiting wasn't all I did and in doing so found myself becoming pregnant with my first child.

Life has a funny way of doing this. Sometimes when all feels lost and there is no one, God has a funny way to show us that life is worth living.

Being pregnant and living with my mom helped me begin my own journey of self-discovery. When I found out I was pregnant, I made the choice to go to college, and find employment. I succeeded both at university and employment but knew I wanted more. It was as if the vision of myself as a younger child would showed back up and I could create a life to be the mother I always dreamt of. Present with the ability to be there for my children.

Six weeks prior to my due date, my mother and I were in a car accident that induced by contractions. After being sent home on bed rest, three days later, my son was born. My son was like an angel to me, after having so much loss it was amazing to see life. Two weeks after delivery, my son stopped breathing in his sleep and was rushed to the hospital. He was given a spinal tap and after testing they diagnosed him with sleep apnea and he was on a breathing monitor for 6 months.

Throughout Micah's development, he would have night terrors and I noticed he wasn't developing like his peers. When I would mention it to his doctors what I noticed that they would tell me was "he'll grow out of it" but he never did. I took it as a way of life and by his second birthday I began my journey as an entrepreneur, plus size model, and pageant queen.

My journey in the entertainment industry was not easy as a single mother, I often found myself battling the time to work a full-time job, follow my dreams and raise a child. When Micah was 4, I made the plunge to quit my job go to school full-time and pursue my dreams as an entrepreneur. During my journey as a fashion marketing student and entrepreneur, I was lucky to be crowned Ms. Illinois Plus America and created an amazing plus size modeling organization called X'Change Modeling. This lead me to bigger opportunities in the industry assisting with production on larger fashion shows. However, life would pause again as I found myself pregnant, and my son was diagnosed with Sensory Processing Disorder.

On the journey of MOM-preneurship there are roadblocks, but it is the human spirit that keeps us persisting without exception. I've learned to trust the pauses in my life and business. While pregnant I was still pushing against the grain but found myself on bedrest. Sick and depressed, I gave up my dream of entrepreneurship and ended up on public assistance, and raising a child alone again. In the midst of it all I was taking my son to Occupational therapy to meet his sensory needs and learning more about Autism Spectrum Disorders. When my son Melech was born, everything in life seem greater. I eventually had a greater purpose for life and again tried to jump back into the entrepreneurial seat as a Zumba instructor. Not only did I find a passion for entrepreneurship again, participating in a documentary for Urban Single MOM-preneurs entitled MOM-preneurs Chicago. I also was preparing to produce my own fashion show, as I found zeal in utilizing my marketing expertise for small businesses. I found joy as I was prepping for my first big event and landing a small internship in a beauty salon. BUT all that ended quickly. As luck would have it, I would find myself pregnant with a third child and had to just STOP trying to pursue my heart's desire.

What was wrong with me, why was I making choices to drain my success? What I've learned from therapy is that sometimes we repeat behavior patterns from places of discontentment. We hide behind the depths of who we think we are, secretly seeking to fulfill a loss needed within ourselves. For me I found myself involved in risky behavior, not thinking of their consequences but risking myself for a temporary satisfying feeling. Not that I would necessarily change the past, I have learned that for every action there is a reaction whether good or bad.

Having to stop yet again another passionate pursuit of my life's desire, I found myself moving in with my mother, on welfare, on bedrest and getting weekly progesterone shots, and in therapy for depression. This was the straw that broke the camel's back: I found myself in a cycle of self-destruction and wasn't sure I would ever be a successful MOM or MOM-preneur. Two weeks after the birth of my daughter I ended up being hospitalized for Suicidal Ideation with a plan, postpartum depression/Psychosis. This begun the journey of reinventing myself.

You never know how strong you are until you've fallen into the depths of darkness in search of the true light within.

After 7 days in the hospital I was ready to restart my life. The road to recovery was bumpy, but I knew that I could do it. I also had a team of cheerleaders to get me through. I used my recovery action plan to make changes for the better, although I did try again to kill myself but my brother was able to be sure it didn't happen. He called me to see if I was ok and while on the phone I told him I was ready to die and would swallow a bottle of pills. He called the local sheriff and I will never forget what he told me. "I'm supposed to take your children and have you committed. But I can't, there is something about you. I know your mom's on the way, but promise me you'll never do this again. Your children need you and you've got to live for them." This was the defining moment that sent me on the blazing path of recovery.

Yes, I still get depressed (we all ebb and flow) and yes, I have ups and downs but I know that my life's worth living.

Nearly 4 months later I found myself writing a book, on the cover of the local paper for teaching free Zumba classes, and becoming a social media virtual assistant. Thus, my passion for helping entrepreneurs and small business executes well and learning tech became my passion. Within this time period I landed my first paid client, a spa in DeKalb Illinois that needed a website and support with marketing. I was so ecstatic and so was my client, and I have been offering a same variation of those business services with the same client ever since. This became the path to a stable life.

Within this period, I noticed my younger children had some developmental differences and self-referred them to early intervention services. It was then that I learned my youngest daughter needed PT for congenital torticollis and my middle son had sensory processing disorder and hearing loss in his right ear. I began advocating for their services all while maintaining my businesses!

I've learned that even when life gets hard you don't have to give up, you move around and flow with the current.

Life did get a lot harder, and in fact I found myself in a deep depression and knew it was time to restart my life. I didn't give up my businesses I put them on pause, because I decided to move across the country to restart my life. With a one week ticket and $5, I took a two-day trip from Illinois to California and restarted my life.

Yes, I leaned into family to make this happen, but taking that leap has been instrumental to the success of who I am today. Within one week of my arrival I landed a full-time job, and was able to have my children and mother here to start the school year. 3 months later, I had my own apartment and one year later my children had updated medical diagnosis including Autism, ADHD, and Sensory Processing Disorder. Was I devastated... NO! Actually, I was glad to finally have answers to my questions and a way to get them the support they needed.

Children with special needs require more direct attention, I have found myself not being able to work a job consistently because of my bouts of deep depression and raising children with different abilities. I've learned I needed to become a full-time MOM-preneur to be able to get them the support they needed and live a better life for our family. Within the last 3 years, I have taken the plunge into online/offline entrepreneurship. I started marketing myself as a virtual assistant, but found myself lost in the shuffle of Internet noise. With no clarity around what I wanted to do with my business, I found myself following every online marketing guru. I downloaded every freebie, opted into everyones mailing list, thinking I could just work their magic formula. It got dome bad that I realize I was on a hamster wheel of financial dissaray and found myself only making $1.50 per day with 5 clients and 3 children.

I decided that the buck stops here! I invested in a great business/marketing coach, and had a mini mastermind of women that could help me figure out my true passion. I found myself being passionate about speaking up about mental health, domestic violence, and empowering women and youth to do MORE of what they love. I also found that I have a passion for working with creatives, therapists, and consultants find sustainable business solutions, systems and strategies that improve their overall wellness and also take the pressure off doing "ALL THE THINGS" in their business.

Once I found my passion, direction and motivation I quickly changed my pricing while prepping to give my clients the news. Talk about walking in fear! Who was I to increase my pricing and change direction? I knew that in order to make this mom-preneur thing work, I had no choice but to be BIG in the world! I lost them all except 1, and became ok with the risk of loss. I learned that in losing the clients that weren't serving me, I gained more ideal clients who helped me operate in my purpose, and my passion. I now run two profitable (more than $1.50 per day) businesses on my terms, helping women find systems, solutions, and strategies to help them Synergize, Focus and Thrive in their everyday life.

Whether you're a veteran MOM-preneur or just starting out remember that your past does not define your future. You are incredible just for simply believing in your ability to raise a family, and run a business. Each day take simple steps to improve on the vision for your life and eventually all the pieces will flow together. There will be speed bumps on the road ahead, but YOU have all the power to ride the bumps and live your best life NOW! I believe in You! Keep Thriving.

# BOOK CONTRIBUTORS

**AYESHA SHAREEF HASHIM**
www.instagram.com/inspiredbymomma

**CIARA MCCARRON**
**REDESIGN YOUR VIBE**
www.facebook.com/redesignyourvibe/

**VICTORIA GAMBLE -**
**HAND CRAFTED BY VICTORIA**
www.instagram.com/hand_crafted_by_victoria_xx

**FILI TAGALOA**

**ANA LOUISE BONASERA -**
**BOOTYCAMP**
www.bootycampltd.com

**DENISE MARTINEZ-ROSSINI**
www.facebook.com/denisemartinezrossini

**LUCY TOLLERFIELD -**
**FOUNDER OF MAMA BLOG MAMAROOANDBOY**
www.mamarooandboy.com

**NAOMI JADE FRANCIS**
**VENUE STYLIST**
www.vintagevenuestyling.co.uk.

**VICKY BARBOUR-ANDREWS**
www.Thebabyexpertssuffolk.co.uk

**VAL BLACKBURN**
**AUTHOR**
http://bit.ly/JasperDragon

**HANNAH JAGO**
www.facebook.com/hannah.jago.3

**HOLLY MATTHEWS**
**ACTRESS**
www.iamhollymatthews.com

**MAGGIE CAVANAGH**
www.facebook.com/maggielcavanagh

**CHRISTINA GEORGIOU**
www.fancydollface.com

**MYISHA HILL MYISHA T**
**LIFE AND BUSINESS SYNERGIST**
www.myishat.com

**KATIE HELLIWELL**
**PSYCHIC MEDIUM**
www.katichclliwellpsychicmedium.com

**SHERRY CANNON JONES**
**SCJGLOBAL**
www.facebook.com/theinspiritedfighterbusiness

**SANDIE COLES**
https://www.facebook.com/sandie.pollardcoles

**LAURA CARLOW**
**FOUNDER/CEO OF BELLE'N'BEAR LTD**
Www.facebook.com/Lauracarlow01

**KATIE COLELLA**
**KATIE COLELLA SOCIAL**
katiecolellasocial.co.uk

Made in the USA
Columbia, SC
26 December 2017